Learning Perl Objects, References, and Modules

Randal L. Schwartz
with Tom Phoenix

O'REILLY®

Beijing · Cambridge · Farnham · Köln · Paris · Sebastopol · Taipei · Tokyo

Learning Perl Objects, References, and Modules
by Randal L. Schwartz with Tom Phoenix

Copyright © 2003 O'Reilly & Associates, Inc. All rights reserved.
Printed in the United States of America.

Published by O'Reilly & Associates, Inc., 1005 Gravenstein Highway North, Sebastopol, CA 95472.

O'Reilly & Associates books may be purchased for educational, business, or sales promotional use. Online editions are also available for most titles (*safari.oreilly.com*). For more information, contact our corporate/institutional sales department: (800) 998-9938 or *corporate@oreilly.com*.

Editor:	Linda Mui
Production Editor:	Mary Anne Weeks Mayo
Cover Designer:	Ellie Volckhausen
Interior Designer:	David Futato

Printing History:

June 2003:   First Edition.

ISBN: 0-596-00478-8

Table of Contents

Foreword ix

Preface xi

1. **Introduction** 1
    What Should You Know Already?   2
    What About All Those Footnotes?   2
    What's with the Exercises?   2
    What if I'm a Perl Course Instructor?   3

2. **Building Larger Programs** 4
    The Cure for the Common Code   4
    Inserting Code with eval   5
    Using do   6
    Using require   8
    require and @INC   9
    The Problem of Namespace Collisions   11
    Packages as Namespace Separators   12
    Scope of a Package Directive   14
    Packages and Lexicals   15
    Exercises   15

3. **Introduction to References** 17
    Performing the Same Task on Many Arrays   17
    Taking a Reference to an Array   19
    Dereferencing the Array Reference   20
    Dropping Those Braces   21
    Modifying the Array   22

Nested Data Structures 23
Simplifying Nested Element References with Arrows 25
References to Hashes 26
Exercises 28

4. References and Scoping **30**
More than One Reference to Data 30
What if That Was the Name? 31
Reference Counting and Nested Data Structures 32
When Reference Counting Goes Bad 34
Creating an Anonymous Array Directly 35
Creating an Anonymous Hash 38
Autovivification 40
Autovivification and Hashes 42
Exercises 44

5. Manipulating Complex Data Structures **45**
Using the Debugger to View Complex Data 45
Viewing Complex Data with Data::Dumper 50
Storing Complex Data with Storable 51
The map and grep Operators 53
Using map 55
Applying a Bit of Indirection 56
Selecting and Altering Complex Data 58
Exercises 59

6. Subroutine References **61**
Referencing a Named Subroutine 61
Anonymous Subroutines 65
Callbacks 67
Closures 68
Returning a Subroutine from a Subroutine 70
Closure Variables as Inputs 73
Closure Variables as Static Local Variables 73
Exercise 75

7. Practical Reference Tricks **77**
Review of Sorting 77
Sorting with Indices 78

Sorting Efficiently   79
The Schwartzian Transform   81
Recursively Defined Data   82
Building Recursively Defined Data   82
Displaying Recursively Defined Data   85
Exercises   86

8. Introduction to Objects **88**
If We Could Talk to the Animals...   89
Introducing the Method Invocation Arrow   90
The Extra Parameter of Method Invocation   91
Calling a Second Method to Simplify Things   92
A Few Notes About @ISA   93
Overriding the Methods   94
Starting the Search from a Different Place   96
The SUPER Way of Doing Things   97
What to Do with @_   97
Where We Are So Far...   97
Exercises   98

9. Objects with Data **99**
A Horse Is a Horse, of Course of Course—or Is It?   99
Invoking an Instance Method   100
Accessing the Instance Data   101
How to Build a Horse   102
Inheriting the Constructor   102
Making a Method Work with Either Classes or Instances   103
Adding Parameters to a Method   104
More Interesting Instances   105
A Horse of a Different Color   106
Getting Your Deposit Back   106
Don't Look Inside the Box   108
Faster Getters and Setters   109
Getters That Double as Setters   109
Restricting a Method to Class-Only or Instance-Only   110
Exercise   110

10. Object Destruction **112**

Beating a Dead Horse   117
Indirect Object Notation   118
Additional Instance Variables in Subclasses   119
Using Class Variables   121
Weakening the Argument   122
Exercise   125

11. Some Advanced Object Topics **126**

UNIVERSAL Methods   126
Testing Your Objects for Good Behavior   127
AUTOLOAD as a Last Resort   128
Using AUTOLOAD for Accessors   129
Creating Getters and Setters More Easily   130
Multiple Inheritance   132
References to Filehandles   133
Exercise   135

12. Using Modules **137**

Sample Function-Oriented Interface: File::Basename   137
Selecting What to Import   138
Sample Object-Oriented Interface: File::Spec   138
A More Typical Object-Oriented Module: Math::BigInt   139
The Differences Between OO and Non-OO Modules   140
What use Is Doing   140
Setting the Path at the Right Time   141
Importing with Exporter   143
@EXPORT and @EXPORT_OK   144
Exporting in a Primarily OO Module   145
Custom Import Routines   147
Exercise   147

13. Writing a Distribution **148**

Starting with h2xs   149
Looking at the Templates   149
The Prototype Module Itself   152
Embedded Documentation   154
Controlling the Distribution withMakefile.PL   158
Alternate Installation Locations (PREFIX=...)   159

Trivial make test   160
Trivial make install   161
Trivial make dist   162
Using the Alternate Library Location   162
Exercise   163

14. Essential Testing **164**
What the Test Harness Does   166
Writing Tests with Test::Simple   167
Writing Tests with Test::More   168
Conditional Tests   172
More Complex Tests (Multiple Test Scripts)   173
Testing Things That Write to STDOUT and STDERR   173
Exercise   174

15. Contributing to CPAN **175**
The Comprehensive Perl Archive Network   175
Getting Prepared   176
Preparing Your Distribution   176
Uploading Your Distribution   177
Announcing the Module   178
Testing on Multiple Platforms   178
Consider Writing an Article or Giving a Talk   178
Exercise   179

Appendix. Answers to Exercises **181**

Index **197**

Foreword

Perl's object-oriented mechanism is classic prestidigitation. It takes a collection of Perl's existing non-OO features such as packages, references, hashes, arrays, subroutines, and modules, and then—with nothing up its sleeve—manages to conjure up fully functional objects, classes, and methods. Seemingly out of nowhere.

That's a great trick. It means you can build on your existing Perl knowledge and ease your way into OO Perl development, without first needing to conquer a mountain of new syntax or navigate an ocean of new techniques. It also means you can progressively fine-tune OO Perl to meet your own needs, by selecting from the existing constructs the one that best suits your task.

But there's a problem. Since Perl co-opts packages, references, hashes, arrays, subroutines, and modules as the basis of its OO mechanism, to use OO Perl you already need to understand packages, references, hashes, arrays, subroutines, and modules.

And there's the rub. The learning curve hasn't been eliminated; it's merely been pushed back half a dozen steps.

So then: how are you going to learn everything you need to know about non-OO Perl so you can start to learn everything you need to know about OO Perl?

This book is the answer. In the following pages, Randal draws on two decades of using Perl, and four decades of watching *Gilligan's Island* and *Mr. Ed,* to explain each of the components of Perl that collectively underpin its OO features. And, better still, he then goes on to show exactly how to combine those components to create useful classes and objects.

So if you still feel like Gilligan when it comes to Perl's objects, references, and modules, this book is just what the Professor ordered.

And that's straight from the horse's mouth.

—Damian Conway
May 2003

Preface

Ten years ago, I wrote the first edition of *Learning Perl*. In the intervening years, Perl itself has grown substantially from a "cool" scripting language used primarily by Unix system administrators to a robust object-oriented programming language that runs on practically every computing platform known to mankind.

Throughout its three editions, *Learning Perl* remained the same size (about 300 pages) and continued to cover much of the same material to remain compact and accessible to the beginning programmer. But there is much more to learn about Perl than there was ten years ago.

This book may be entitled *Learning Perl Objects, References, and Modules*, but I like to think of it as just *Learning More Perl.** This is the book that picks up where *Learning Perl* leaves off. It shows how to use Perl to write larger programs.

As in *Learning Perl*, each chapter in this book is designed to be small enough to read in just an hour or two. Each chapter ends with a series of exercises to help you practice what you've just learned, with the answers in the Appendix for your reference. And like *Learning Perl*, the material in this book was developed for a teaching environment and used in that setting, including for our own use at Stonehenge Consulting Services as we present onsite and open-enrollment trainings.

You don't have to be a Unix guru, or even a Unix user, to benefit from this book. Unless otherwise noted, everything in this book applies equally well to Windows ActivePerl from ActiveState, and all other modern implementations of Perl. To use this book, you just need to be familiar with the material in *Learning Perl* and have the ambition to go further.

---

* Don't ask why it isn't called that. We must have had 30 emails on the subject.

Structure of This Book

It's a good idea to read this book from front to back, stopping to do the exercises. Each chapter builds on preceding chapters. You've been warned.

Chapter 1, *Introduction*
> An introduction to the material.

Chapter 2, *Building Larger Programs*
> How to bring code in from separate files so you can have others do some of your work for you.

Chapter 3, *Introduction to References*
> How to allow the same code to operate on different data structures by introducing a level of indirection.

Chapter 4, *References and Scoping*
> How Perl manages to keep track of pointers to data, and an introduction to anonymous data structures and autovivification.

Chapter 5, *Manipulating Complex Data Structures*
> Viewing, searching, and storing nested arrays and hashes.

Chapter 6, *Subroutine References*
> How to capture behavior as a value to be passed around.

Chapter 7, *Practical Reference Tricks*
> Sorting complex operations, the "Schwartzian Transform," and working with recursively defined data.

Chapter 8, *Introduction to Objects*
> Working with classes, method calls, inheritance, and overriding.

Chapter 9, *Objects with Data*
> Adding per-instance data, including constructors, getters, and setters.

Chapter 10, *Object Destruction*
> Adding behavior to an object that is going away, including object persistence.

Chapter 11, *Some Advanced Object Topics*
> Multiple inheritance, automatic methods, and references to filehandles.

Chapter 12, *Using Modules*
> How use works, from the user's and author's perspectives.

Chapter 13, *Writing a Distribution*
> Packaging up a module for sharing, including portable installation instructions.

Chapter 14, *Essential Testing*
> Providing unit and integration tests with your distribution.

Chapter 15, *Contributing to CPAN*
> Submitting your module to the CPAN.

Appendix, *Answers to Exercises*
> Where to go to get answers.

Conventions Used in This Book

The following typographic conventions are used in this book:

Constant width
> Used for function names, module names, filenames, environment variables, code snippets, and other literal text

Italics
> Used for emphasis and for new terms where they are defined

Comments and Questions

Please address comments and questions concerning this book to the publisher:

O'Reilly & Associates, Inc.
1005 Gravenstein Highway North
Sebastopol, CA 95472
(800) 998-9938 (in the United States or Canada)
(707) 829-0515 (international/local)
(707) 829-0104 (fax)

There is a web page for this book, which lists errata, examples, or any additional information. You can access this page at:

> *http://www.oreilly.com/catalog/lrnperlorm*

To comment or ask technical questions about this book, send email to:

> *bookquestions@oreilly.com*

For more information about books, conferences, Resource Centers, and the O'Reilly Network, see the O'Reilly web site at:

> *http://www.oreilly.com*

Acknowledgments

In the preface of the first edition of *Learning Perl*, I acknowledged the Beaverton McMenamin's Cedar Hills Pub just down the street from my house for the "rent-free booth-office space" while I wrote most of the draft on my Powerbook 140. Well, like wearing your lucky socks every day when your favorite team is in the playoffs, I wrote nearly all of this book (including these words) at the same brewpub, in hopes that the light of success of the first book will shine on me twice.

This McM's has the same great local microbrew beer and greasy sandwiches, but they've gotten rid of my favorite pizza bread, replacing it with new items like marionberry cobbler (a local treat) and spicy jambalaya. (And they added two booths, and put in some pool tables.) Also, instead of the Powerbook 140, I'm using a Titanium Powerbook, with 1,000 times more disk, 500 times more memory, and a 200-times-faster CPU running a real Unix-based operating system (OSX) instead of the limited MacOS. I also uploaded all of the draft sections (including this one) over my 144K cell-phone modem and emailed them directly to the reviewers, instead of having to wait to rush home to my 9600-baud external modem and phone line. How times have changed!

So, thanks once again to the staff of the McMenamin's Cedar Hills Pub for the booth space and hospitality.

Like the third edition of *Learning Perl*, I also owe much of what I'm saying here and how I'm saying it to the decade of students at Stonehenge Consulting Services who have given me immediate precise feedback (by their glazed eyes and awkwardly constructed questions) when I was exceeding the "huh?" factor threshold. With that feedback over many dozens of presentations, I was able to keep refining and refactoring the materials that paved the way for this book.

Speaking of which, those materials started as a half-day "What's new in Perl 5?" summary commissioned by Margie Levine of Silicon Graphics, in addition to my frequently presented onsite four-day Llama course (targeted primarily for Perl Version 4 at the time). Eventually, I got the idea to beef up those notes into a full course and enlisted fellow Stonehenge presenter Joseph Hall for the task. (He's the one that selected the universe from which the examples are drawn.) Joseph developed a two-day course for Stonehenge in parallel with his excellent *Effective Perl Programming* book, which we then used as the course textbook (until now).

Other Stonehenge instructors have also dabbled a bit in the "Packages, References, Objects, and Modules" course over the years, including Chip "every source line of the Perl compiler memorized" Salzenberg, "don't mess with my name" brian d foy, and Tad "something clever this way comes" McClellan. But the bulk of the recent changes has been the responsibility of my senior trainer Tom Phoenix, who has been "Stonehenge employee of the month" so often that I may have to finally give up my preferred parking space. Tom manages the materials (just as Tad manages operations) so I can focus on being the president and the janitor of Stonehenge. And since I'm naming the Stonehenge crew, I can't forget my wacky party manager and marketing consultant (and longtime friend) Bill Harp, who at this very moment is planning yet another legendary Stonehenge OSCON party (including the premiere of the book you're now reading).

Tom Phoenix contributed most exercises in this book and a timely set of review notes during my writing process, including entire paragraphs for me to just insert in place of the drivel I had written. We work well as a team, both in the classroom and in our joint writing efforts. It is for this effort that we've acknowledged Tom as a coauthor, but I'll take direct blame for any parts of the book you end up hating: none of that could have possibly been Tom's fault.

I also appreciate my technical reviewers, Mike Stok, Joe Johnston, Paul Grassie, Damian Conway, Neil Bauman, and David H. Adler, for their constructive feedback and kind words, although I really was expecting to be beat up a bit more in the comments. Maybe the time limit kept y'all nice.

And I especially appreciate and acknowledge Linda Mui of O'Reilly, who has shepherded this project through from the beginning, when Tom and I suggested at OSCON 2001 that our next book should be a sequel, and then made it so.

Of course, a book is nothing without a subject and a distribution channel, and for that I must acknowledge longtime associates Larry Wall and Tim O'Reilly. Thanks guys, for creating an industry that has paid for my toys and essentials for over a decade.

And, as always, a special thanks to Lyle and Jack for teaching me nearly everything I know about writing and convincing me that I was much more than a programmer who might learn to write: I was also a writer who happened to know how to program. Thank you.

And to you, the reader of this book, for whom I toiled away the countless hours while sipping a cold microbrew and scarfing down a piece of incredible cheesecake, trying to avoid spilling on my laptop keyboard: thank you for reading what I've written. I sincerely hope I've contributed (in at least a small way) to your Perl proficiency. If you ever meet me on the street, please say "Hi."* I'd like that. Thank you.

---

* And yes, you can ask a Perl question at the same time. I don't mind.

## CHAPTER 1

Introduction

Welcome to next step in your understanding of Perl. You're probably here either because you want to learn to write programs that are more than 100 lines long or because your boss has told you to do so.

See, our *Learning Perl* book was great because it introduced the use of Perl for short and medium programs (which is most of the programming done in Perl, we've observed). But, to avoid having "the Llama book" be as big and intimidating as "the Camel book," we left a lot of information out, deliberately and carefully.

In the pages that follow, you can get "the rest of the story" in the same style as our friendly Llama book. It covers what you need to write programs that are 100 to 10,000 lines long.

For example, you'll learn how to work with multiple programmers on the same project. This is great, because unless you work 35 hours each day, you'll need some help with larger tasks. You'll also need to ensure that your code all fits with the other code as it is developed for the final application.

This book will also show you how to deal with larger and more complex data structures, such as what we might casually call a "hash of hashes" or an "array of arrays of hashes of arrays."

And then there's the buzzworthy notion of object-oriented programming, which allows parts of your code (or hopefully code from others) to be reused with minor or major variations within the same program. The book will cover that as well, even if you've never seen objects before.

An important aspect of working in teams is having a release cycle and tests for unit and integration testing. You'll learn the basics of packaging your code as a distribution and providing unit tests for that distribution, both for development and for verifying that your code works in the ultimate end environment.

Hopefully, just as was promised and delivered in *Learning Perl*, you'll be entertained along the way by interesting examples and bad puns. (We've sent Fred and Barney and Betty and Wilma home, though. A new cast of characters will take the starring roles.)

What Should You Know Already?

We'll presume that you've already read *Learning Perl,* or at least pretend you have, and that you've played enough with Perl to already have those basics down. For example, you won't see an explanation in this book that shows how to access the elements of an array or return a value from a subroutine.

Make sure you know the following things:

- How to run a Perl program on your system
- Scalars
- Arrays
- Hashes
- Control structures such as while, if, for, and foreach
- Subroutines
- Perl operators such as grep, map, sort, and print
- File manipulation such as open, file reading, and -x (file tests)

You might pick up deeper insight into these topics in this book, but we're going to presume you know the basics.

What About All Those Footnotes?

Like *Learning Perl,* this book relegates some of the more esoteric items out of the way for the first reading and places those items in footnotes.[*] You should skip those the first time through and pick them up on a rereading. You will not find anything in a footnote that is needed to understand any of the later material.

What's with the Exercises?

Hands-on training gets the job done better. The best way to provide this training is with a series of one or more exercises after every half-hour to hour of presentation. Of course, if you're a speed reader, the end of the chapter may come a bit sooner than a half hour. Slow down. Take a breather. But do the exercises.

Each exercise has a "minutes to complete" rating. This rating hits the midpoint of the bell curve but don't feel bad if you take significantly longer or shorter. Some-

---

[*] Like this.

times it's just a matter of how many times you've faced similar programming tasks in your studies or jobs. Use the numbers merely as a guideline.

Every exercise has its answer in the Appendix. Again, try not to peek; you'll ruin the value of the exercise.

What if I'm a Perl Course Instructor?

If you're a Perl instructor who has decided to use this as your textbook, you should know that each set of exercises is short enough for most students to complete the whole set in 45 minutes to an hour, with a little time left over for a break. Some chapters' exercises should be quicker, and some may take longer. That's because once all those little numbers in square brackets were written, we discovered that we don't know how to add.

So let's get started. Class begins after you turn the page...

CHAPTER 2
Building Larger Programs

This chapter looks at how to break up a program into pieces and includes some of the concerns that arise when you put those pieces back together again, or when many people work together on the same program.

The Cure for the Common Code

Let's say a famous sailor (we'll call him "the Skipper") uses Perl to help navigate his ocean-going vessel (call it "the Minnow"). The Skipper writes many Perl programs to provide navigation for all the common ports of call for the Minnow. He finds himself cutting and pasting a very common routine into each program:

```
sub turn_towards_heading {
  my $new_heading = shift;
  my $current_heading = current_heading();
  print "Current heading is ", $current_heading, ".\n";
  print "Come about to $new_heading ";
  my $direction = "right";
  my $turn = ($new_heading - $current_heading) % 360;
  if ($turn > 180) { # long way around
    $turn = 360 - $turn;
    $direction = "left";
  }
  print "by turning $direction $turn degrees.\n";
}
```

This routine gives the shortest turn to make from the current heading (returned by the subroutine current_heading()) to a new heading (given as the first parameter to the subroutine).

The first line of this subroutine might have read instead:

```
  my ($new_heading) = @_;
```

This is mostly a style call: in both cases, the first parameter ends up in $new_heading. However, in later chapters, you'll see that removing the items from @_ as they are identified does have some advantages. So, this book sticks (mostly) with the "shifting" style of argument parsing. Now back to the matter at hand...

Suppose that after having written a dozen programs using this routine, the Skipper realizes that the output is excessively chatty when he's already taken the time to steer the proper course (or perhaps simply started drifting in the proper direction). After all, if the current heading is 234 degrees and he needs to turn to 234 degrees, you see:

```
Current heading is 234.
Come about to 234 by turning right 0 degrees.
```

How annoying! The Skipper decides to fix this problem by checking for a zero turn value:

```perl
sub turn_towards_heading {
  my $new_heading = shift;
  my $current_heading = current_heading();
  print "Current heading is ", $current_heading, ".\n";
  my $direction = "right";
  my $turn = ($new_heading - $current_heading) % 360;
  unless ($turn) {
    print "On course (good job!).\n";
    return;
  }
  print "Come about to $new_heading ";
  if ($turn > 180) { # long way around
    $turn = 360 - $turn;
    $direction = "left";
  }
  print "by turning $direction $turn degrees.\n";
}
```

Great. The new subroutine works nicely in the current navigation program. However, because it had previously been cut-and-pasted into a half dozen other navigation programs, those other programs will still annoy the Skipper with extraneous turning messages.

You need a way to write the code in one place and then share it among many programs. And like most things in Perl, there's more than one way to do it.

Inserting Code with eval

The Skipper can save disk space (and brainspace) by bringing the definition for turn_towards_heading out into a separate file. For example, suppose the Skipper figures out a half-dozen common subroutines related to navigating the Minnow that he seems to use in most or all of the programs he's writing for the task. He can put them in a separate file called navigation.pl, which consists only of the needed subroutines.

But now, how can you tell Perl to pull in that program snippet from another file? You could do it the hard way:

```
sub load_common_subroutines {
  open MORE_CODE, "navigation.pl" or die "navigation.pl: $!";
  undef $/; # enable slurp mode
  my $more_code = <MORE_CODE>;
  close MORE_CODE;
  eval $more_code;
  die $@ if $@;
}
```

The code from `navigation.pl` is read into the `$more_code` variable. You then use `eval` to process that text as Perl code. Any lexical variables in `$more_code` will remain local to the evaluated code.[*] If there's a syntax error, the `$@` variable is set and causes the subroutine to `die` with the appropriate error message.

Now instead of a few dozen lines of common subroutines to place in each file, you simply have one subroutine to insert in each file.

But that's not very nice, especially if you need to keep doing this kind of task repeatedly. Luckily, there's (at least) one Perl built-in to help you out.

Using do

The Skipper has placed a few common navigation subroutines into `navigation.pl`. If the Skipper merely inserts:

```
do "navigation.pl";
die $@ if $@;
```

into his typical navigation program, it's almost the same as if the eval code were executed earlier.[†]

That is, the `do` operator acts as if the code from `navigation.pl` were incorporated into the current program, although in its own scope block so that lexicals (`my` variables) and most directives (such as `use strict`) from the included file don't leak into the main program.

Now the Skipper can safely update and maintain only one copy of the common subroutines, without having to copy and recopy all the fixes and extensions into the many separate navigation programs he is creating and using. See Figure 2-1 for an illustration.

Of course, this requires a bit of discipline because breaking the expected interface of a given subroutine will now break many programs instead of just one.[‡] Careful

---

[*] Oddly, the variable `$more_code` is also visible to the evaluated code, not that it is of any use to change that variable during the `eval`.

[†] Except in regard to `@INC`, `%INC`, and missing file handling, which you'll see later.

[‡] In later chapters, you'll see how to set up tests to be used while maintaining reused code.

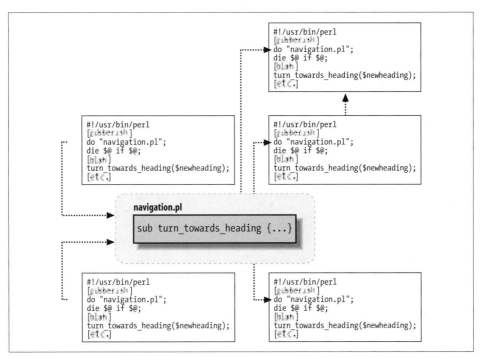

Figure 2-1. The navigation.pl file being used by the other navigation programs

thought will need to be given as to how to design and write reusable components and modular design. We'll presume The Skipper has had some experience at that.

Another advantage to placing some of the code into a separate file is that other programmers can reuse the Skipper's routines and vice versa. For example, suppose the Skipper's sidekick (we'll call him "Gilligan") writes a routine to drop_anchor( ) and places it in the file drop_anchor.pl.* Then, the Skipper can use the code with:

```
do "drop_anchor.pl";
die $@ if $@;
...
drop_anchor( ) if at_dock( ) or in_port( );
```

Thus, the code is brought into separate files to permit easy maintenance and interprogrammer cooperation.

---

* The .pl here stands for "perl library," the common extension used for included Perl code. It is unfortunate that some non-Unix Perl vendors also use to use the same extension for the top-level Perl programs, because you then can't tell whether something is a program or a library. If you have a choice, the experts recommend ending your program filenames with .plx ("Perl executable"), or better yet, with no extension at all unless your system requires one.

While the code brought in from a .pl file can have direct executable statements, it's much more common to simply define subroutines that can be called by the code containing the do.

Going back to that drop_anchor.pl library for a second, imagine what would happen if the Skipper wrote a program that needed to "drop anchor" as well as navigate:

```
do "drop_anchor.pl";
die $@ if $@;
do "navigate.pl";
die $@ if $@;
...
turn_towards_heading(90);
...
drop_anchor( ) if at_dock( );
```

That works fine and dandy. The subroutines defined in both libraries are available to this program.

Using require

Suppose navigate.pl itself also pulls in drop_anchor.pl for some common navigation task. You'll end up reading the file once directly, and then again while processing the navigation package. This will needlessly redefine drop_anchor( ). Worse than that, if warnings are enabled,* you'll get a warning from Perl that you've redefined the subroutine, even though it's the same definition.

What you need is a mechanism that tracks what files have been brought in and bring them in only once. Perl has such an operation, called require. Change the previous code to simply:

```
require "drop_anchor.pl";
require "navigate.pl";
```

The require operator keeps track of the files it has read.† Once a file has been processed successfully, any further require operations on that same file are simply ignored. This means that even if navigate.pl contains require "drop_anchor.pl", the drop_anchor.pl file is brought in exactly once, and you'll get no annoying error messages about duplicate subroutine definitions (see Figure 2-2). Most importantly, you'll also save time by not processing the file more than once .

The require operator also has two additional features:

- Any syntax error in the required file causes the program to die, thus the many die $@ if $@ statements are unnecessary.
- The last expression evaluated in the file must return a true value.

---

* You *are* using warnings, right? You can enable them with either -w or use warnings;.

† In the %INC hash, as described in the entry for require in the perlfunc documentation.

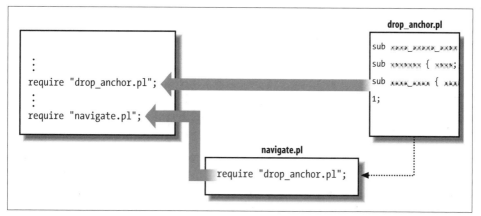

Figure 2-2. Once the drop_anchor.pl file is brought in, another attempt to require the file is harmless

Because of the second point, most files evaluated for require have a cryptic 1; as their last line of code. This ensures that the last evaluated expression is in fact true. Try to carry on this tradition as well.

Originally, the mandatory true value was intended as a way for an included file to signal to the invoker that the code was processed successfully and that no error condition existed. However, nearly everyone has adopted the die if ... strategy instead, deeming the "last expression evaluated is false" strategy a mere historic annoyance.

require and @INC

So far, the examples have glossed over the directory structure of where the main code and the included files (either with do or require) are located. That's because it "just works" for the simplest case, in which you have a program and its libraries in the same directory, and you run the program from that directory.

Things get a bit more complicated when the libraries aren't located in the current directory. In fact, Perl searches for libraries along a library search path (similar to what the shell does with the PATH environment variable). The current directory (represented in Unix by a single dot) is an element of the search path, so as long as your libraries are in your current working directory, everything is fine.

The search path is given in the special @INC array. By default, the array contains the current directory and a half-dozen directories built in to the perl binary during the compilation of perl itself. You can see what these directories are by typing perl -V at the command line and noting the last dozen lines of the output. Also at the command line, you can execute the following to get just the @INC directories:[*]

```
perl -le 'print for @INC'
```

---

[*] On a Windows machine, use double quotes instead of single quotes on the command line.

Except for . in that list, you probably won't be able to write to any of the other directories, unless you're the person responsible for maintaining Perl on your machine, in which case you should be able to write to all of them. The remaining directories are where Perl searches for system-wide libraries and modules, as you'll see later.

Extending @INC

Although you may not be able to alter the content of the directories named by @INC, you can alter @INC itself before the require, to bring in libraries from one or more directories of your choosing. The @INC array is an ordinary array, so have the Skipper add a directory below his home directory to the mix:

```
unshift @INC, "/home/skipper/perl-lib";
```

Now, in addition to searching the standard directories and the current directory, Perl searches the Skipper's personal Perl library. In fact, Perl searches in that directory first, since it is the first one in @INC. By using unshift rather than push, any conflict in names between the Skipper's private files and the system-installed files are resolved with the Skipper's file taking precedence.

Extending @INC with PERL5LIB

The Skipper must edit each program that uses the private libraries to include this line. If that seems like too much editing, the Skipper can instead set the PERL5LIB environment variable to the directory name. For example, in the C shell, it'd be:

```
setenv PERL5LIB /home/skipper/perl-lib
```

In Bourne-style shells, it'd be something like:

```
PERL5LIB=/home/skipper/perl-lib; export PERL5LIB
```

The advantage of using PERL5LIB is that the Skipper can set it once and forget it. The disadvantage comes when someone else (like Gilligan) comes along to execute the program. Unless Gilligan has also added the same PERL5LIB environment variable, the program will fail! Thus, while PERL5LIB is interesting for personal use, do not rely on it for programs you intend to share with others. (And don't make your entire team of programmers add a common PERL5LIB variable. That's just wrong.)

The PERL5LIB variable can include multiple directories, separated by colons. Any specified directory is inserted at the beginning of @INC.

While a system administrator might add a setting of PERL5LIB to a system-wide startup script, this process is generally frowned upon. The purpose of PERL5LIB is to enable nonadministrators to extend Perl to recognize additional directories. If a system administrator wants additional directories, he merely needs to recompile and reinstall Perl, answering the appropriate questions during the configuration phase.

Extending @INC with -I

If Gilligan recognizes that one of the Skipper's programs is missing the proper directive, Gilligan can either add the proper PERL5LIB variable or invoke perl directly with one or more -I options. For example, to invoke the Skipper's get_us_home program, the command line might be something like:

```
perl -I/home/skipper/perl-lib /home/skipper/bin/get_us_home
```

Or use -I cmd line option

Obviously, it's easier for Gilligan if the program itself defines the extra libraries. But sometimes just adding a -I fixes things right up.*

This works even if Gilligan can't edit the Skipper's program. He still has to be able to read it, of course, but Gilligan can use this technique to try a new version of his library with the Skipper's program, for example.

The Problem of Namespace Collisions

Suppose that the Skipper has added all his cool and useful routines to navigation.pl and that Gilligan has incorporated the library into his own navigation package head_ towards_island:

```perl
#!/usr/bin/perl

require 'navigation.pl';

sub turn_toward_port {
  turn_toward_heading(compute_heading_to_island());
}

sub compute_heading_to_island {
  .. code here ..
}

.. more program here ..
```

Gilligan then has his program debugged (perhaps with the aid of a smart person whom we'll call "the Professor"), and everything works well.

However, now the Skipper decides to modify his navigation.pl library, adding a routine called turn_toward_port that makes a 45-degree turn toward the left (known as "port" in nautical jargon).

Gilligan's program will fail in a catastrophic way, as soon as he tries to head to port: he'll start steering the ship in circles! The problem is that the Perl compiler first compiles turn_toward_port from Gilligan's main program, then when the require is

---

* Extending @INC with either PERL5LIB or -I also automatically adds the version- and architecture-specific subdirectories of the specified directories. Adding these directories automatically simplifies the task of installing Perl modules that include architecture- or version-sensitive components, such as compiled C code.

evaluated at runtime, the definition for turn_toward_port is redefined as the Skipper's definition. Sure, if Gilligan has warnings enabled, he'll notice something is wrong, but why should he have to count on that?

The problem is that Gilligan defined turn_toward_port as meaning "turn toward the port on the island," while the Skipper defined it as "turn toward the left." How do you resolve this?

One way is to require that the Skipper put an explicit prefix in front of every name defined in the library, say navigation_. Thus, Gilligan's program ends up looking like:

```
#!/usr/bin/perl

require 'navigation.pl';

sub turn_toward_port {
  navigation_turn_toward_heading(compute_heading_to_island());
}

sub compute_heading_to_island {
  .. code here ..
}

.. more program here ..
```

Clearly, the navigation_turn_toward_heading comes from the navigation.pl file. This is great for Gilligan, but awkward for the Skipper, as his file now becomes:

```
sub navigation_turn_toward_heading {
  .. code here ..
}

sub navigation_turn_toward_port {
  .. code here ..
}

1;
```

Yes, every scalar, array, hash, filehandle, or subroutine now has to have a navigation_ prefix in front of it to guarantee that the names won't collide with any potential users of the library. Obviously, for that old sailor, this ain't gonna float his boat. So, what do you do instead?

Packages as Namespace Separators

If the name prefix of the last example didn't have to be spelled out on every use, things would work much better. Well, you can improve the situation by using a package:

```
package Navigation;

sub turn_towards_heading {
```

```
   .. code here ..
}

sub turn_towards_port {
  .. code here ..
}

1;
```

The package declaration at the beginning of this file tells Perl to insert Navigation:: in front of most names within the file: Thus, the code above practically says:

```
sub Navigation::turn_towards_heading {
  .. code here ..
}

sub Navigation::turn_towards_port {
  .. code here ..
}

1;
```

Now when Gilligan uses this file, he simply adds Navigation:: to the subroutines defined in the library, and leaves the Navigation:: prefix off for subroutines he defines on his own:

```
#!/usr/bin/perl

require 'navigation.pl';

sub turn_toward_port {
  Navigation::turn_toward_heading(compute_heading_to_island( ));
}

sub compute_heading_to_island {
  .. code here ..
}

.. more program here ..
```

Package names are like variable names: they consist of alphanumerics and underscores, as long as you don't begin with a digit. Also, for reasons explained in the perlmodlib documentation, a package name should begin with a capital letter and not overlap an existing CPAN or core module name. Package names can also consist of multiple names separated by double colons, such as Minnow::Navigation and Minnow::Food::Storage.

Nearly every scalar, array, hash, subroutine, and filehandle name[*] is actually prefixed by the current package, unless the name already contains one or more double-colon markers. So, in navigation.pl, you can use variables such as:

[*] Except lexicals, as you'll see in a moment.

```
package Navigation;
@homeport = (21.1, -157.525);

sub turn_toward_port {
  .. code ..
}
```

(Trivia note: 21.1 degrees north, 157.525 degrees west is the location of the real-life marina where the opening shot of a famous television series was filmed.)

You can refer to the @homeport variable in the main code as:

```
@destination = @Navigation::homeport;
```

If every name has a package name inserted in front of it, what about names in the main program? Yes, they are also in a package, called main. It's as if package main; were at the beginning of each file. Thus, to keep Gilligan from having to say Navigation::turn_towards_heading, the navigation.pl file can say:

```
sub main::turn_towards_heading {
  .. code here ..
}
```

Now the subroutine is defined in the main package, not the Navigation package. This isn't an optimal solution (you'll see better solutions in Chapter 12), but at least there's nothing sacred or terribly unique about main compared to any other package.

Scope of a Package Directive

All files start as if you had said package main;. Any package directive remains in effect until the next package directive, unless that package directive is inside a curly-braced scope. In that case, the prior package is remembered and restored when the scope ends. Here's an example:

```
package Navigation;

{  # start scope block
  package main;  # now in package main

  sub turn_towards_heading {  # main::turn_towards_heading
    .. code here ..
  }

}  # end scope block

# back to package Navigation

sub turn_towards_port { # Navigation::turn_towards_port
  .. code here ..
}
```

The current package is lexically scoped, similar to the scope of my variables, narrowed to the innermost-enclosing brace pair or file in which the package is introduced.

Most libraries have only one package declaration at the top of the file. Most programs leave the package at the default main package. However it's nice to know that you can temporarily have a different current package.*

Packages and Lexicals

A lexical variable (a variable introduced with my) isn't prefixed by the current package because package variables are always *global*: you can always reference a package variable if you know its full name. A lexical variable is usually temporary and accessible for only a portion of the program. If a lexical variable is declared, then using that name without a package prefix results in accessing the lexical variable. However, a package prefix ensures that you are accessing a package variable and never a lexical variable.

For example, suppose a subroutine within navigation.pl declares a lexical @homeport variable. Any mention of @homeport will then be the newly introduced lexical variable, but a fully qualified mention of @Navigation::homeport accesses the package variable instead.

```
package Navigation;
@homeport = (21.1, -157.525);

sub get_me_home {
  my @homeport;

  .. @homeport .. # refers to the lexical variable
  .. @Navigation::homeport .. # refers to the package variable

}

.. @homeport .. # refers to the package variable
```

Obviously, this can lead to confusing code, so you shouldn't introduce such a duplication needlessly. The results are completely predictable, though.

Exercises

The answers for all exercises can be found in the Appendix.

Exercise 1 [30 min]

The Oogaboogoo natives on the island have unusual names for the days and months. Here is some simple but not very well-written code from Gilligan. Fix it up, add a

---

* Some names are always in package main regardless of the current package: ARGV, ARGVOUT, ENV, INC, SIG, STDERR, STDIN, and STDOUT. You can always refer to @INC and be assured of getting @main::INC. The punctuation mark variables such as $_, $2, and $! are either all lexicals or forced into package main, so when you write $. you never get $Navigation::. by mistake.

conversion function for the month names, and make the whole thing into a library. For extra credit, add suitable error checking and consider what should be in the documentation.

```
@day = qw(ark dip wap sen pop sep kir);
sub number_to_day_name { my $num = shift @_; $day[$num]; }
@month = qw(diz pod bod rod sip wax lin sen kun fiz nap dep);
```

Exercise 2 [10 min]

Make a program that uses your library and the following code to print out a message, such as Today is dip, sen 11, 2008, meaning that today is a Monday in August. (Hint: The year and month numbers returned by localtime may not be what you'd expect, so you need to check the documentation.)

```
my($sec, $min, $hour, $mday, $mon, $year, $wday) = localtime;
```

## CHAPTER 3

Introduction to References

A Perl scalar variable holds a single value. An array holds an ordered list of one or more scalars. A hash holds a collection of scalars as values, keyed by other scalars.

Although a scalar can be an arbitrary string, which allows complex data to be encoded into an array or hash, none of the three data types are well-suited to complex data interrelationships. This is a job for the *reference*. Let's look at the importance of references by starting with an example.

Performing the Same Task on Many Arrays

Before the Minnow can leave on an excursion (e.g., a three-hour tour), every passenger and crew member should be checked to ensure they have all the required trip items in their possession. Let's say that for maritime safety, every person on board the Minnow needs to have a life preserver, some sunscreen, a water bottle, and a rain jacket. You can write a bit of code to check for the Skipper's supplies:

```
my @required = qw(preserver sunscreen water_bottle jacket);
my @skipper = qw(blue_shirt hat jacket preserver sunscreen);
for my $item (@required) {
  unless (grep $item eq $_, @skipper) { # not found in list?
    print "skipper is missing $item.\n";
  }
}
```

The grep in a scalar context returns the number of times the expression $item eq $_ returns true, which is 1 if the item is in the list and 0 if not.* If the value is 0, it's false, and you print the message.

---

* There are more efficient ways to check list membership for large lists, but for a few items, this is probably the easiest way to do so with just a few lines of code.

Of course, if you want to check on Gilligan and the Professor, you might write the following code:

```perl
my @gilligan = qw(red_shirt hat lucky_socks water_bottle);
for my $item (@required) {
  unless (grep $item eq $_, @gilligan) { # not found in list?
    print "gilligan is missing $item.\n";
  }
}

my @professor = qw(sunscreen water_bottle slide_rule batteries radio);
for my $item (@required) {
  unless (grep $item eq $_, @professor) { # not found in list?
    print "professor is missing $item.\n";
  }
}
```

You may start to notice a lot of repeated code here and decide that it would be served best in a subroutine:

```perl
sub check_required_items {
  my $who = shift;
  my @required = qw(preserver sunscreen water_bottle jacket);
  for my $item (@required) {
    unless (grep $item eq $_, @_) { # not found in list?
      print "$who is missing $item.\n";
    }
  }
}

my @gilligan = qw(red_shirt hat lucky_socks water_bottle);
check_required_items("gilligan", @gilligan);
```

The subroutine is given five items in its @_ array initially: the name gilligan and the four items belonging to Gilligan. After the shift, @_ will have only the items. Thus, the grep checks each required item against the list.

So far, so good. You can check the Skipper and the Professor with just a bit more code:

```perl
my @skipper = qw(blue_shirt hat jacket preserver sunscreen);
my @professor = qw(sunscreen water_bottle slide_rule batteries radio);
check_required_items("skipper", @skipper);
check_required_items("professor", @professor);
```

And for the other passengers, you repeat as needed. Although this code meets the initial requirements, you've got two problems to deal with:

- To create @_, Perl copies the entire contents of the array to be scanned. This is fine for a few items, but if the array is large, it seems a bit wasteful to copy the data just to pass it into a subroutine.

- Suppose you want to modify the original array to force the provisions list to include the mandatory items. Because you have a copy in the subroutine ("pass by value"), any changes made to @_ aren't reflected automatically in the corresponding provisions array.[*]

To solve either or both of these problems, you need pass by reference rather than pass by value. And that's just what the doctor (or Professor) ordered.

Taking a Reference to an Array

Among its many other meanings, the backslash (\) character is also the "take a reference to" operator. When you use it in front of an array name, e.g., \@skipper, the result is a *reference* to that array. A reference to the array is like a pointer: it points at the array, but is not the array itself.

A reference fits wherever a scalar fits. It can go into an element of an array or a hash, or into a plain scalar variable, like this:

```
my $reference_to_skipper = \@skipper;
```

The reference can be copied:

```
my $second_reference_to_skipper = $reference_to_skipper;
```

or even:

```
my $third_reference_skipper = \@skipper;
```

All three references are completely interchangeable. You can even say they're identical:

```
if ($reference_to_skipper == $second_reference_to_skipper) {
  print "They are identical references.\n";
}
```

This equality compares the numeric forms of the two references. The numeric form of the reference is the unique memory address of the @skipper internal data structure, unchanging during the life of the variable. If you look at the string form instead, with eq or print, you get a debugging string:

```
ARRAY(0x1a2b3c)
```

which again is unique for this array because it includes the hexadecimal (base 16) representation of the array's unique memory address. The debugging string also notes that this is an array reference. Of course, if you ever see something like this in your output, it almost certainly means there's a bug; users of your program have little interest in hex dumps of storage addresses!

---

[*] Actually, assigning new scalars to elements of @_ after the shift modifies the corresponding variable being passed, but that still wouldn't let you extend the array with additional mandatory provisions.

Because a reference can be copied, and passing an argument to a subroutine is really just copying, you can use this code to pass a reference to the array into the subroutine:

```
my @skipper = qw(blue_shirt hat jacket preserver sunscreen);
check_required_items("The Skipper", \@skipper);

sub check_required_items {
  my $who = shift;
  my $items = shift;
  my @required = qw(preserver sunscreen water_bottle jacket);
  ...
}
```

Now $items in the subroutine will be a reference to the array of @skipper. But how do you get from a reference back into the original array? By *dereferencing* the reference.

Dereferencing the Array Reference

If you look at @skipper, you'll see that it consists of two parts: the @ symbol and the name of the array. Similarly, the syntax $skipper[1] consists of the name of the array in the middle and some syntax around the outside to get at the second element of the array (index value 1 is the second element because you start counting index values at 0).

Here's the trick: any reference to an array can be placed in curly braces and written in place of the name of an array, ending up with a method to access the original array. That is, wherever you write skipper to name the array, you use the reference inside curly braces: { $items }. For example, both of these lines refer to the entire array:

```
@  skipper
@{ $items }
```

whereas both of these refer to the second item of the array:*

```
$  skipper [1]
${ $items }[1]
```

By using the reference form, you've decoupled the code and the method of array access from the actual array. Let's see how that changes the rest of this subroutine:

```
sub check_required_items {
  my $who = shift;
  my $items = shift;
  my @required = qw(preserver sunscreen water_bottle jacket);
  for my $item (@required) {
    unless (grep $item eq $_, @{$items}) { # not found in list?
```

---

* Note that whitespace was added in these two displays to make the similar parts line up. This whitespace is legal in a program, even though most programs won't use it.

```
      print "$who is missing $item.\n";
    }
  }
}
```

All you did was replace @_ (the copy of the provisions list) with @{$items}, a dereferencing of the reference to the original provisions array. Now you can call the subroutine a few times as before:

```
my @skipper = qw(blue_shirt hat jacket preserver sunscreen);
check_required_items("The Skipper", \@skipper);
my @professor = qw(sunscreen water_bottle slide_rule batteries radio);
check_required_items("Professor", \@professor);
my @gilligan = qw(red_shirt hat lucky_socks water_bottle);
check_required_items("Gilligan", \@gilligan);
```

In each case, $items points to a different array, so the same code applies to different arrays each time it is invoked. This is one of the most important uses of references: decoupling the code from the data structure on which it operates so the code can be reused more readily.

Passing the array by reference fixes the first of the two problems mentioned earlier. Now, instead of copying the entire provision list into the @_ array, you get a single element of a reference to that provisions array.

Could you have eliminated the two shifts at the beginning of the subroutine? Sure, at the expense of clarity:

```
sub check_required_items {
  my @required = qw(preserver sunscreen water_bottle jacket);
  for my $item (@required) {
    unless (grep $item eq $_, @{$_[1]}) { # not found in list?
      print "$_[0] is missing $item.\n";
    }
  }
}
```

You still have two elements in @_. The first element is the passenger or crew member name and is used in the error message. The second element is a reference to the correct provisions array, used in the grep expression.

Dropping Those Braces

Most of the time, the dereferenced array reference is contained in a simple scalar variable, such as @{$items} or ${$items}[1]. In those cases, the curly braces can be dropped, unambiguously, forming @$items or $$items[1].

However, the braces cannot be dropped if the value within the braces is not a simple scalar variable. For example, for @{$_[1]} from that last subroutine rewrite, you can't remove the braces.

This rule also means that it's easy to see where the "missing" braces need to go. When you see $$items[1], a pretty noisy piece of syntax, you can tell that the curly braces must belong around the simple scalar variable, $items. Therefore, $items must be a reference to an array.

Thus, an easier-on-the-eyes version of that subroutine might be:

```
sub check_required_items {
  my $who = shift;
  my $items = shift;
  my @required = qw(preserver sunscreen water_bottle jacket);
  for my $item (@required) {
    unless (grep $item eq $_, @$items) { # not found in list?
      print "$who is missing $item.\n";
    }
  }
}
```

The only difference here is that the braces were removed for @$items.

Modifying the Array

You've seen how to solve the excessive copying problem with an array reference. Now let's look at modifying the original array.

For every missing provision, push that provision onto an array, forcing the passenger to consider the item:

```
sub check_required_items {
  my $who = shift;
  my $items = shift;
  my @required = qw(preserver sunscreen water_bottle jacket);
  my @missing = ( );

  for my $item (@required) {
    unless (grep $item eq $_, @$items) { # not found in list?
      print "$who is missing $item.\n";
      push @missing, $item;
    }
  }

  if (@missing) {
    print "Adding @missing to @$items for $who.\n";
    push @$items, @missing;
  }
}
```

Note the addition of the @missing array. If you find any items missing during the scan, push them into @missing. If there's anything there at the end of the scan, add it to the original provision list.

The key is in the last line of that subroutine. You're dereferencing the $items array reference, accessing the original array, and adding the elements from @missing. Without passing by reference, you'd modify only a local copy of the data, which has no effect on the original array.

Also, @$items (and its more generic form @{$items}) works within a double-quoted string. Do not include any whitespace between the @ and the immediately following character, although you can include nearly arbitrary whitespace within the curly braces as if it were normal Perl code.

Nested Data Structures

In this example, the array @_ contains two elements, one of which is also an array. What if you take a reference to an array that also contains a reference to an array? You end up with a complex data structure, which can be quite useful.

For example, iterate over the data for the Skipper, Gilligan, and the Professor by first building a larger data structure holding the entire list of provision lists:

```
my @skipper = qw(blue_shirt hat jacket preserver sunscreen);
my @skipper_with_name = ("Skipper", \@skipper);
my @professor = qw(sunscreen water_bottle slide_rule batteries radio);
my @professor_with_name = ("Professor", \@professor);
my @gilligan = qw(red_shirt hat lucky_socks water_bottle);
my @gilligan_with_name = ("Gilligan", \@gilligan);
```

At this point, @skipper_with_name has two elements, the second of which is an array reference, similar to what was passed to the subroutine. Now group them all:

```
my @all_with_names = (
  \@skipper_with_name,
  \@professor_with_name,
  \@gilligan_with_name,
);
```

Note that you have just three elements, each of which is a reference to an array, each of which has two elements: the name and its corresponding initial provisions. A picture of that is in Figure 3-1.

Therefore, $all_with_names[2] will be the array reference for the Gilligan's data. If you dereference it as @{$all_with_names[2]}, you get a two-element array, "Gilligan" and another array reference.

How would you access that array reference? Using your rules again, it's ${$all_with_names[2]}[1]. In other words, taking $all_with_names[2], you dereference it in an expression that would be something like $DUMMY[1] as an ordinary array, so you'll place {$all_with_names[2]} in place of DUMMY.

How do you call the existing check_required_items( ) with this data structure? The following code is easy enough.

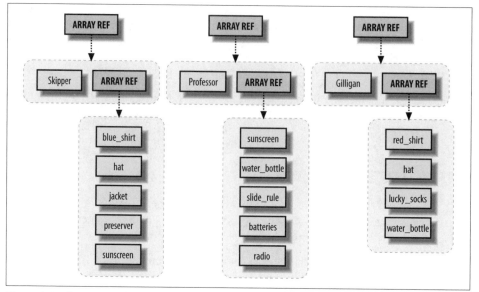

Figure 3-1. The array @all_with_names holds a multilevel data structure containing strings and references to arrays

```
for my $person (@all_with_names) {
  my $who = $$person[0];
  my $provisions_reference = $$person[1];
  check_required_items($who, $provisions_reference);
}
```

This requires no changes to the subroutine. $person will be each of $all_with_names[0], $all_with_names[1], and $all_with_names[2], as the loop progresses. When you dereference $$person[0], you get "Skipper," "Professor," and "Gilligan," respectively. $$person[1] is the corresponding array reference of provisions for that person.

Of course, you can shortcut this as well, since the entire dereferenced array matches the argument list precisely:

```
for my $person (@all_with_names) {
  check_required_items(@$person);
}
```

or even:

```
check_required_items(@$_) for @all_with_names;
```

As you can see, various levels of optimization can lead to obfuscation. Be sure to consider where your head will be a month from now when you have to reread your own code. If that's not enough, consider the new person who takes over your job after you have left.

Simplifying Nested Element References with Arrows

Look at the curly-brace dereferencing again. As in the earlier example, the array reference for Gilligan's provision list is `${$all_with_names[2]}[1]`. Now, what if you want to know Gilligan's first provision? You need to dereference *this* item one more level, so it's Yet Another Layer of Braces: `${${$all_with_names[2]}[1]}[0]`. That's a really noisy piece of syntax. Can you shorten that? Yes!

Everywhere you write `${DUMMY}[$y]`, you can write `DUMMY->[$y]` instead. In other words, you can dereference an array reference, picking out a particular element of that array by simply following the expression defining the array reference with an arrow and a square-bracketed subscript.

For this example, this means you can pick out the array reference for Gilligan with a simple `$all_with_names[2]->[1]`, and Gilligan's first provision with `$all_with_names[2]->[1]->[0]`. Wow, that's definitely easier on the eyes.

If *that* wasn't already simple enough, there's one more rule: if the arrow ends up between "subscripty kinds of things," like square brackets, you can also drop the arrow. `$all_with_names[2]->[1]->[0]` becomes `$all_with_names[2][1][0]`. Now it's looking even easier on the eye.

The arrow has to be *between* subscripty things. Why wouldn't it be between? Well, imagine a reference to the array `@all_with_names`:

```
my $root = \@all_with_names;
```

Now how do you get to Gilligan's first item?

```
$root -> [2] -> [1] -> [0]
```

More simply, using the "drop arrow" rule, you can use:

```
$root -> [2][1][0]
```

You cannot drop the first arrow, however, because that would mean an array `@root`'s third element, an entirely unrelated data structure. Let's compare this to the full curly-brace form again:

```
${${${$root}[2]}[1]}[0]
```

It looks much better with the arrow. Note, however, that no shortcut gets the entire array from an array reference. If you want all of Gilligan's provisions, you say:

```
@{$root->[2][1]}
```

Reading this from the inside out, you can think of it like this:

1. Take $root.
2. Dereference it as an array reference, taking the third element of that array (index number 2).

3. Dereference that as an array reference, taking the second element of that array (index number 1).

4. Dereference that as an array reference, taking the entire array.

The last step doesn't have a shortcut arrow form. Oh well.[*]

References to Hashes

Just as you can take a reference to an array, you can also take a reference to a hash. Once again, you use the backslash as the "take a reference to" operator:

```
my %gilligan_info = (
  name => 'Gilligan',
  hat => 'White',
  shirt => 'Red',
  position => 'First Mate',
);
my $hash_ref = \%gilligan_info;
```

You can dereference a hash reference to get back to the original data. The strategy is similar to dereferencing an array reference. Write the hash syntax as you would have without references, and then replace the name of the hash with a pair of curly braces surrounding the thing holding the reference. For example, to pick a particular value for a given key, use:

```
my $name = $ gilligan_info { 'name' };
my $name = $ { $hash_ref } { 'name' };
```

In this case, the curly braces have two different meanings. The first pair denotes the expression returning a reference, while the second pair delimits the expression for the hash key.

To perform an operation on the entire hash, you proceed similarly:

```
my @keys = keys % gilligan_info;
my @keys = keys % { $hash_ref };
```

As with array references, you can use shortcuts to replace the complex curly-braced forms under some circumstances. For example, if the only thing inside the curly braces is a simple scalar variable (as shown in these examples so far), you can drop the curly braces:

```
my $name = $$hash_ref{'name'};
my @keys = keys %$hash_ref;
```

Like an array reference, when referring to a specific hash element, you can use an arrow form:

```
my $name = $hash_ref->{'name'};
```

---

[*] It's not that it hasn't been discussed repeatedly by the Perl developers; it's just that nobody has come up with a nice backward-compatible syntax with universal appeal.

Because a hash reference fits wherever a scalar fits, you can create an array of hash references:

```perl
my %gilligan_info = (
  name => 'Gilligan',
  hat => 'White',
  shirt => 'Red',
  position => 'First Mate',
);
my %skipper_info = (
  name => 'Skipper',
  hat => 'Black',
  shirt => 'Blue',
  position => 'Captain',
);
my @crew = (\%gilligan_info, \%skipper_info);
```

Thus, $crew[0] is a hash reference to the information about Gilligan. You can get to Gilligan's name via any one of:

```perl
${ $crew[0] } { 'name' }
my $ref = $crew[0]; $$ref{'name'}
$crew[0]->{'name'}
$crew[0]{'name'}
```

On that last one, you can still drop the arrow between "subscripty kinds of things," even though one is an array bracket and one is a hash brace.

Let's print a crew roster:

```perl
my %gilligan_info = (
  name => 'Gilligan',
  hat => 'White',
  shirt => 'Red',
  position => 'First Mate',
);
my %skipper_info = (
  name => 'Skipper',
  hat => 'Black',
  shirt => 'Blue',
  position => 'Captain',
);
my @crew = (\%gilligan_info, \%skipper_info);

my $format = "%-15s %-7s %-7s %-15s\n";
printf $format, qw(Name Shirt Hat Position);
for my $crewmember (@crew) {
  printf $format,
    $crewmember->{'name'},
    $crewmember->{'shirt'},
    $crewmember->{'hat'},
    $crewmember->{'position'};
}
```

That last part looks very repetitive. You can shorten it with a hash slice. Again, if the original syntax is:

```
@ gilligan_info { qw(name position) }
```

the hash slice notation from a reference looks like:

```
@ { $hash_ref } { qw(name position) }
```

You can drop the first brace pair because the only thing within is a simple scalar value, yielding:

```
@ $hash_ref { qw(name position) }
```

Thus, you can replace that final loop with:

```
for my $crewmember (@crew) {
  printf $format, @$crewmember{qw(name shirt hat position)};
}
```

There is no shortcut form with an arrow (->) for array slices or hash slices, just as there is no shortcut for entire arrays or hashes.

A hash reference prints as a string that looks like HASH(0x1a2b3c), showing the hexa-decimal memory address of the hash. That's not very useful to an end user and only barely more usable to the programmer, except as an indication of the lack of appro-priate dereferencing.

Exercises

The answers for all exercises can be found in the Appendix.

Exercise 1 [5 min]

How many different things do these expressions refer to?

```
$ginger->[2][1]
${$ginger[2]}[1]
$ginger->[2]->[1]
${$ginger->[2]}[1]
```

Exercise 2 [30 min]

Using the final version of check_required_items, write a subroutine check_items_for_ all that takes a hash reference as its only parameter, pointing at a hash whose keys are the people aboard the Minnow, and whose corresponding values are array refer-ences of the things they intend to bring on board.

For example, the hash reference might be constructed like so:

```
my @gilligan = ... gilligan items ...;
my @skipper = ... skipper items ...;
my @professor = ... professor items ...;
```

```
my %all = (
  "Gilligan" => \@gilligan,
  "Skipper" => \@skipper,
  "Professor" => \@professor,
);
check_items_for_all(\%all);
```

The newly constructed subroutine should call check_required_items for each person in the hash, updating their provisions list to include the required items.

CHAPTER 4

References and Scoping

References can be copied and passed around like any other scalar. At any given time, Perl knows the number of references to a particular data item. Perl can also create references to *anonymous data structures* (structures that do not have explicit names) and create references automatically as needed to fulfill certain kinds of operations. Let's look at copying references and how it affects scoping and memory usage.

More than One Reference to Data

Chapter 3 explored how to take a reference to an array @skipper and place it into a new scalar variable:

```
my @skipper = qw(blue_shirt hat jacket preserver sunscreen);
my $reference_to_skipper = \@skipper;
```

You can then copy the reference or take additional references, and they'd all refer to the same thing and be interchangeable:

```
my $second_reference_to_skipper = $reference_to_skipper;
my $third_reference_to_skipper = \@skipper;
```

At this point, you have four different ways to access the data contained in @skipper:

```
@skipper
@$reference_to_skipper
@$second_reference_to_skipper
@$third_reference_to_skipper
```

Perl tracks how many ways the data can be accessed through a mechanism called *reference counting*. The original name counts as one, and each additional reference that was taken (including copies of references) also counts as one. The total number of references to the array of provisions is now four.

You can add and remove references as you wish, and as long as the reference count doesn't hit zero, the array is maintained in memory and is still accessible via any of the other access paths. For example, you might have a temporary reference:

```
check_provisions_list(\@skipper)
```

When this subroutine begins executing, a fifth reference to the data is created and copied into @_ for the subroutine. The subroutine is free to create additional copies of that reference, which Perl notes as needed. Typically, when the subroutine returns, all such references are discarded automatically, and you're back to four references again.

You can kill off each reference by using the variable for something other than a reference to the value of @skipper. For example, you can assign undef to the variable:

```
$reference_to_skipper = undef;
```

Or, maybe just let the variable go out of scope:

```
my @skipper = ...;
{
  ...
  my $ref = \@skipper;
  ...
  ...
} # $ref goes out of scope at this point
```

In particular, a reference held in a subroutine's private (lexical) variable goes away at the end of the subroutine.

Whether the value is changed or the variable itself goes away, Perl notes it as an appropriate reduction in the number of references to the data.

Perl recycles the memory for the array only when all references (including the name of the array) go away. In this case, memory is reclaimed when @skipper goes out of scope, as well as all other references that had been taken to @skipper are removed or modified to be another value. Such memory is available to Perl for other data later in this program invocation but generally will not be returned to the operating system for use by other processes.

What if That Was the Name?

Typically, all references to a variable are removed before the variable itself. But what if one of the references outlives the variable name? For example, consider this code:

```
my $ref;
{
  my @skipper = qw(blue_shirt hat jacket preserver sunscreen);
  $ref = \@skipper;
  print "$ref->[2]\n"; # prints jacket\n
}
print "$ref->[2]\n"; # still prints jacket\n
```

Immediately after the @skipper array is declared, you have one reference to the five-element list. After $ref is initialized, you'll have two, down to the end of the block. When the block ends, the @skipper name disappears. However, this was only one of the two ways to access the data! Thus, the five-element list is not removed from memory, and $ref is still pointing to that data.

At this point, the five-element list is contained within an *anonymous array*, which is a fancy term for an array without a name.

Until the value of $ref is changed, or $ref itself disappears, you can still continue to use all the dereferencing strategies you used prior to when the name of the array disappeared. In fact, it's still a fully functional array that you can shrink or grow just as you do any other Perl array:

```
push @$ref, "sextant"; # add a new provision
print "$ref->[-1]\n"; # prints sextant\n
```

You can even increase the reference count at this point:

```
my $copy_of_ref = $ref;
```

or equivalently:

```
my $copy_of_ref = \@$ref;
```

The data remains alive until the last reference is destroyed:

```
$ref = undef; # not yet...
$copy_of_ref = undef; # poof!
```

Reference Counting and Nested Data Structures

The data remains alive until the last reference is destroyed, even if that reference is contained within a larger active data structure. Suppose an array element is itself a reference. Recall the example from Chapter 3:

```
my @skipper = qw(blue_shirt hat jacket preserver sunscreen);
my @skipper_with_name = ("The Skipper", \@skipper);
my @professor = qw(sunscreen water_bottle slide_rule batteries radio);
my @professor_with_name = ("The Professor", \@professor);
my @gilligan = qw(red_shirt hat lucky_socks water_bottle);
my @gilligan_with_name = ("Gilligan", \@gilligan);
my @all_with_names = (
  \@skipper_with_name,
  \@professor_with_name,
  \@gilligan_with_name,
);
```

Imagine for a moment that the intermediate variables are all part of a subroutine:

```
my @all_with_names;

sub initialize_provisions_list {
  my @skipper = qw(blue_shirt hat jacket preserver sunscreen);
  my @skipper_with_name = ("The Skipper", \@skipper);
  my @professor = qw(sunscreen water_bottle slide_rule batteries radio);
```

```
    my @professor_with_name = ("The Professor", \@professor);
    my @gilligan = qw(red_shirt hat lucky_socks water_bottle);
    my @gilligan_with_name = ("Gilligan", \@gilligan);
    @all_with_names = ( # set global
      \@skipper_with_name,
      \@professor_with_name,
      \@gilligan_with_name,
    );
}

initialize_provisions_list();
```

The value of @all_with_names is set to contain three references. Inside the subroutine are named arrays with references to arrays first placed into other named arrays. Eventually, the values end up in the global @all_with_names. However, as the subroutine returns, the names for the six arrays disappear. Each array has had one other reference taken to it, making the reference count temporarily two, and then back to one as the name is removed. Because the reference count is not yet zero, the data continues to live on, although it is now referenced only by elements of @all_with_names.

Rather than assign the global variable, you can rewrite this as:

```
sub get_provisions_list {
  my @skipper = qw(blue_shirt hat jacket preserver sunscreen);
  my @skipper_with_name = ("The Skipper", \@skipper);
  my @professor = qw(sunscreen water_bottle slide_rule batteries radio);
  my @professor_with_name = ("The Professor", \@professor);
  my @gilligan = qw(red_shirt hat lucky_socks water_bottle);
  my @gilligan_with_name = ("Gilligan", \@gilligan);
  return (
    \@skipper_with_name,
    \@professor_with_name,
    \@gilligan_with_name,
  );
}

my @all_with_names = get_provisions_list();
```

Here, you create the value that will eventually be stored into @all_with_names as the last expression evaluated in the subroutine. A three-element list is returned and assigned. As long as the named arrays within the subroutine have had at least one reference taken of them, and it is still part of the return value, the data remains alive.[*]

If the references in @all_with_names are altered or discarded, the reference count for the corresponding arrays is reduced. If that means the reference count has become zero (as in this example), those arrays themselves are also eliminated. Because these arrays also contain a reference (such as the reference to @skipper), that reference is

---

[*] Compare this with having to return an array from a C function. Either a pointer to a static memory space must be returned, making the subroutine nonreentrant, or a new memory space must be malloc'ed, requiring the caller to know to free the data. Perl just does the right thing.

also reduced by one. Again, that reduces the reference count to zero, freeing that memory as well, in a cascading effect.

Removing the top of a tree of data generally removes all the data contained within. The exception is when additional copies are made of the references of the nested data. For example, if you copied Gilligan's provisions:

```
my $gilligan_stuff = $all_with_names[2][1];
```

then when you remove @all_with_names, you still have one live reference to what was formerly @gilligan, and the data from there downward remains alive.

The bottom line is simply: Perl does the right thing. If you still have a reference to data, you still have the data.

When Reference Counting Goes Bad

Reference-counting as a way to manage memory has been around for a long time. The downside of reference counting is that it breaks when the data structure is not a *directed graph*, in which some parts of the structure point back in to other parts in a looping way. For example, suppose each of two data structures contains a reference to the other (see Figure 4-1):

```
my @data1 = qw(one won);
my @data2 = qw(two too to);
push @data2, \@data1;
push @data1, \@data2;
```

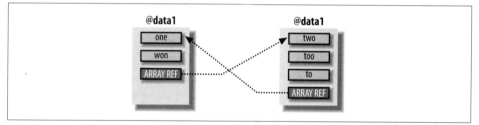

Figure 4-1. When the references in a data structure form a loop, Perl's reference-counting system may not be able to recognize and recycle the no-longer-needed memory space

At this point, there are two names for the data in @data1: @data1 itself and @{$data2[3]}, and two names for the data in @data2: @data2 itself and @{$data1[2]}. You've created a loop. In fact, you can access won with an infinite number of names, such as $data1[2][3][2][3][2][3][1].

What happens when these two array names go out of scope? Well, the reference count for the two arrays goes down from two to one. But not zero! And because it's not zero, Perl thinks there might still be a way to get to the data, even though there isn't! Thus, you've created a *memory leak*. Ugh. (A memory leak in a program causes the program to consume more and more memory over time.)

At this point, you're right to think that example is contrived. Of course you would never make a looped data structure in a real program! Actually, programmers often make these loops as part of doubly-linked lists, linked rings, or a number of other data structures. The key is that Perl programmers rarely do so because the most important reasons to use those data structures don't apply in Perl. If you've used other languages, you may have noticed programming tasks that are comparatively easy in Perl. For example, it's easy to sort a list of items or to add or remove items, even in the middle of the list. Those tasks are difficult in some other languages, and using a looped data structure is a common way to get around the language's limitations.

Why mention it here? Well, even Perl programmers sometimes copy an algorithm from another programming language. There's nothing inherently wrong with doing this, although it would be better to decide why the original author used a "loopy" data structure and recode the algorithm to use Perl's strengths. Perhaps a hash should be used instead, or perhaps the data should go into an array that will be sorted later.

A future version of Perl is likely to use *garbage collection* in addition to or instead of referencing counting. Until then, you must be careful to not create circular references, or if you do, break the circle before the variables go out of scope. For example, the following code doesn't leak:

```
{
  my @data1 = qw(one won);
  my @data2 = qw(two too to);
  push @data2, \@data1;
  push @data1, \@data2;
  ... use @data1, @data2 ...
  # at the end:
  @data1 = ( );
  @data2 = ( );
}
```

You have eliminated the reference to @data2 from within @data1, and vice versa. Now the data has only one reference each, which are returned to zero references at the end of the block. In fact, you can clear out either one and not the other, and it still works nicely. Chapter 10 shows how to create weak references, which can help with many of these problems.

Creating an Anonymous Array Directly

In the get_provisions_list routine earlier, you created a half dozen array names that were used only so that you could take a reference to them immediately afterward. When the subroutine exited, the array names all went away, but the references remained.

While creating temporarily named arrays would work in the simplest cases, creating such names becomes more complicated as the data structures become more detailed.

You'd have to keep thinking of names of arrays just so you can forget them shortly thereafter.

You can reduce the namespace clutter by narrowing down the scope of the various array names. Rather than letting them be declared within the scope of the subroutine, you can create a temporary block:

```perl
my @skipper_with_name;
{
  my @skipper = qw(blue_shirt hat jacket preserver sunscreen);
  @skipper_with_name = ("The Skipper", \@skipper);
}
```

At this point, the second element of @skipper_with_name is a reference to the array formerly known as @skipper. However, the name is no longer relevant.

This is a lot of typing to simply say "the second element should be a reference to an array containing these elements." You can create such a value directly using the *anonymous array constructor*, which is Yet Another Use for square brackets:

```perl
my $ref_to_skipper_provisions =
  [ qw(blue_shirt hat jacket preserver sunscreen) ];
```

The square brackets take the value within (evaluated in a list context); establish a new, anonymous array initialized to those values; and (here's the important part) return a reference to that array. It's as if you said:

```perl
my $ref_to_skipper_provisions;
{
  my @temporary_name =
  ( qw(blue_shirt hat jacket preserver sunscreen) );
  $ref_to_skipper_provisions = \@temporary_name;
}
```

Here you don't need to come up with a temporary name, and you don't need the extra noise of the temporary block. The result of a square-bracketed anonymous array constructor is an array reference, which fits wherever a scalar variable fits.

Now you can use it to construct the larger list:

```perl
my $ref_to_skipper_provisions =
  [ qw(blue_shirt hat jacket preserver sunscreen) ];
my @skipper_with_name = ("The Skipper", $ref_to_skipper_provisions);
```

Of course, you didn't actually need that scalar temporary, either. You can put a scalar reference to an array as part of a larger list:

```perl
my @skipper_with_name = (
  "The Skipper",
  [ qw(blue_shirt hat jacket preserver sunscreen) ]
);
```

Now let's walk through this. You've declared @skipper_with_name, the first element of which is the Skipper's name string, and the second element is an array reference, obtained by placing the five provisions into an array and taking a reference to it. So @skipper_with_name is only two elements long, just as before.

Don't confuse the square brackets with the parentheses here. They each have their distinct purpose. If you replace the square brackets with parentheses, you end up with a six-element list. If you replace the outer parentheses (on the first and last lines) with square brackets, you construct an anonymous array that's two elements long and then take the reference to that array as the only element of the ultimate @skipper_with_name array.*

So, in summary, the syntax:

```perl
my $fruits;
{
  my @secret_variable = ('pineapple', 'papaya', 'mango');
  $fruits = \@secret_variable;
}
```

can be simply replaced with:

```perl
my $fruits = ['pineapple', 'papaya', 'mango'];
```

Does this work for more complicated structures? Yes! Any time you need an element of a list to be a reference to an array, you can create that reference with an anonymous array constructor. In fact, you can also nest them in your provisions list:

```perl
sub get_provisions_list {
  return (
    ["The Skipper",
      [qw(blue_shirt hat jacket preserver sunscreen)]
    ],
    ["The Professor",
      [qw(sunscreen water_bottle slide_rule batteries radio)]
    ],
    ["Gilligan",
      [qw(red_shirt hat lucky_socks water_bottle)]
    ],
  );
}

my @all_with_names = get_provisions_list();
```

Walking through this from the outside in, you have a return value of three elements. Each element is an array reference, pointing to an anonymous two-element array. The first element of each array is a name string, while the second element is a reference to an anonymous array of varying lengths naming the provisions—all without having to come up with temporary names for any of the intermediate layers.

---

* In classrooms, we've seen that too much indirection (or not enough indirection) tends to contribute to the most common mistakes made when working with references.

To the caller of this subroutine, the return value is identical to the previous version. However, from a maintenance point of view, the reduced clutter of not having all the intermediate names saves screen and brain space.

You can show a reference to an empty anonymous hash using an empty anonymous array constructor. For example, if you add one "Mrs. Howell" to that fictional travel list, as someone who has packed rather light, you'd simply insert:

```
["Mrs. Howell",
  []
],
```

This is a single element of the larger list. This item is a reference to an array with two elements, the first of which is the name string, and the second of which is itself a reference to an empty anonymous array. The array is empty because Mrs. Howell hasn't packed anything for this trip.

Creating an Anonymous Hash

Similar to creating an anonymous array, you can also create an anonymous hash. Consider the crew roster from Chapter 3:

```
my %gilligan_info = (
  name => 'Gilligan',
  hat => 'White',
  shirt => 'Red',
  position => 'First Mate',
);
my %skipper_info = (
  name => 'Skipper',
  hat => 'Black',
  shirt => 'Blue',
  position => 'Captain',
);
my @crew = (\%gilligan_info, \%skipper_info);
```

The variables %gilligan_info and %skipper_info are just temporaries, needed to create the hashes for the final data structure. You can construct the reference directly with the *anonymous hash constructor*, which is Yet Another Meaning for curly braces, as you'll see. Replace this:

```
my $ref_to_gilligan_info;
{
  my %gilligan_info = (
    name => 'Gilligan',
    hat => 'White',
    shirt => 'Red',
    position => 'First Mate',
  );
  $ref_to_gilligan_info = \%gilligan_info;
}
```

with the anonymous hash constructor:

```perl
my $ref_to_gilligan_info = {
  name => 'Gilligan',
  hat => 'White',
  shirt => 'Red',
  position => 'First Mate',
};
```

The value between the open and closing curly braces is an eight-element list. The eight-element list becomes a four-element anonymous hash (four key-value pairs). A reference to this hash is taken and returned as a single scalar value, which is placed into the scalar variable. Thus, you cam rewrite the roster creation as:

```perl
my $ref_to_gilligan_info = {
  name => 'Gilligan',
  hat => 'White',
  shirt => 'Red',
  position => 'First Mate',
};
my $ref_to_skipper_info = {
  name => 'Skipper',
  hat => 'Black',
  shirt => 'Blue',
  position => 'Captain',
};
my @crew = ($ref_to_gilligan_info, $ref_to_skipper_info);
```

As before, you can now avoid the temporary variables and insert the values directly into the top-level list:

```perl
my @crew = (
  {
    name => 'Gilligan',
    hat => 'White',
    shirt => 'Red',
    position => 'First Mate',
  },
  {
    name => 'Skipper',
    hat => 'Black',
    shirt => 'Blue',
    position => 'Captain',
  },
);
```

Note the use of trailing commas on the lists when the element is not immediately next to the closing brace, bracket, or parenthesis. This is a nice style element to adopt because it allows for easy maintenance. Lines can be added quickly, rearranged, or commented out without destroying the integrity of the list.

Now @crew is identical to the value it had before, but you no longer need to invent names for the intermediate data structures. As before, the @crew variable contains two elements, each of which is a reference to a hash containing keyword-based information about a particular crew member.

The anonymous hash constructor always evaluates its contents in a list context and then constructs a hash from key/value pairs, just as if you had assigned that list to a named hash. A reference to that hash is returned as a single value that fits wherever a scalar fits.

Now, a word from our parser: because blocks and anonymous hash constructors both use curly braces in roughly the same places in the syntax tree, the compiler has to make ad hoc determinations about which of the two you mean. If the compiler ever decides incorrectly, you might need to provide a hint to get what you want. To show the compiler that you want an anonymous hash constructor, put a plus sign before the opening curly brace: +{ ... }. To be sure to get a block of code, just put a semicolon (representing an empty statement) at the beginning of the block: {; ... }.

Autovivification

Let's look again at the provisions list. Suppose you were reading the data from a file, in the format:

```
The Skipper
  blue_shirt
  hat
  jacket
  preserver
  sunscreen
Professor
  sunscreen
  water_bottle
  slide_rule
Gilligan
  red_shirt
  hat
  lucky_socks
  water_bottle
```

Provisions are indented with some whitespace, following a nonindented line with the person's name. Let's construct a hash of provisions. The keys of the hash will be the person's name, and the value will be an array reference to an array containing a list of provisions.

Initially, you might gather the data using a simple loop:

```
my %provisions;
my $person;
while (<>) {
  if (/^(\S.*)/) { # a person's name (no leading whitespace)
    $person = $1;
    $provisions{$person} = [ ] unless exists $provisions{$person};
  } elsif (/^\s+(\S.*)/) { # a provision
```

```
          die "No person yet!" unless defined $person;
          push @{ $provisions{$person} }, $1;
        } else {
          die "I don't understand: $_";
        }
      }
    }
```

First, you declare the variables for the resulting hash of provisions and the current
person. For each line that is read, determine if it's a person or a provision. If it's a
person, remember the name and create the hash element for that person. The unless
exists test ensures that you won't delete someone's provision list if his list is split in
two places in the data file. For example, suppose that "The Skipper" and " sextant"
(note the leading whitespace) are at the end of the data file in order to list an additional data item.

The key is the person's name, and the value is initially a reference to an empty
anonymous array. If the line is a provision, push it to the end of the correct array,
using the array reference.

This code works fine, but it actually says more than it needs to. Why? Because you
can leave out the line that initializes the hash element's value to a reference to an
empty array:

```
    my %provisions;
    my $person;
    while (<>) {
      if (/^(\S.*)/) { # a person's name (no leading whitespace)
        $person = $1;
        ## $provisions{$person} = [ ] unless exists $provisions{$person};
      } elsif (/^\s+(\S.*)/) { # a provision
        die "No person yet!" unless defined $person;
        push @{ $provisions{$person} }, $1;
      } else {
        die "I don't understand: $_";
      }
    }
```

What happens when you try to store that blue shirt for the Skipper? While looking at
the second line of input, you'll end up with this effect:

```
    push @{ $provisions{"The Skipper"} }, "blue_shirt";
```

At this point, $provisions{"The Skipper"} doesn't exist, but you're trying to use it as
an array reference. To resolve the situation, Perl automatically inserts a reference to a
new empty anonymous array into the variable and continues the operation. In this
case, the reference to the newly created empty array is dereferenced, and you push
the blue shirt to the provisions list.

This process is called *autovivification*. Any nonexisting variable, or a variable containing undef, which is dereferenced while looking for a variable location (technically called *an lvalue context*), is automatically stuffed with the appropriate reference
to an empty item, and the operation is allowed to proceed.

This is actually the same behavior you've probably been using in Perl all along. Perl creates new variables as needed. Before that statement, $provisions{"The Skipper"} didn't exist, so Perl created it. Then @{ $provisions{"The Skipper"} } didn't exist, so Perl created it as well.

For example, this works:

```
my $not_yet;                  # new undefined variable
@$not_yet = (1, 2, 3);
```

Here, you dereference the value $not_yet as if it were an array reference. But since it's initially undef, Perl acts as if you had said:

```
my $not_yet;
$not_yet = [ ]; # inserted through autovivification
@$not_yet = (1, 2, 3);
```

In other words, an initially empty array becomes an array of three elements.

This autovivification also works for multiple levels of assignment:

```
my $top;
$top->[2]->[4] = "lee-lou";
```

Initially, $top contains undef, but because it is dereferenced as if it were an array reference, Perl inserts a reference to an empty anonymous array into $top. The third element (index value 2) is then accessed, which causes Perl to grow the array to be three elements long. That element is also undef, so it is stuffed with a reference to another empty anonymous array. We then spin out along that newly created array, setting the fifth element to lee-lou.

Autovivification and Hashes

Autovivification also works for hash references. If a variable containing undef is dereferenced as if it were a hash reference, a reference to an empty anonymous hash is inserted, and the operation continues.

One place this comes in very handy is in a typical data reduction task. For example let's say the Professor gets an island-area network up and running (perhaps using Coco-Net or maybe Vines), and now wants to track the traffic from host to host. He begins logging the number of bytes transferred to a log file, giving the source host, the destination host, and the number of transferred bytes:

```
professor.hut gilligan.crew.hut 1250
professor.hut lovey.howell.hut 910
thurston.howell.hut lovey.howell.hut 1250
professor.hut lovey.howell.hut 450
professor.hut laser3.copyroom.hut 2924
ginger.girl.hut professor.hut 1218
ginger.girl.hut maryann.girl.hut 199
...
```

Now the Professor wants to produce a summary of the source host, the destination host, and the total number of transferred bytes for the day. Tabulating the data is as simple as:

```
my %total_bytes;
while (<>) {
  my ($source, $destination, $bytes) = split;
  $total_bytes{$source}{$destination} += $bytes;
}
```

Let's see how this works on the first line of data. You'll be executing:

```
$total_bytes{"professor.hut"}{"gilligan.crew.hut"} += 1250;
```

Because %total_bytes is initially empty, the first key of professor.hut is not found, but it establishes an undef value for the dereferencing as a hash reference. (Keep in mind that an implicit arrow is between the two sets of curly braces here.) Perl sticks in a reference to an empty anonymous hash in that element, which then is immediately extended to include the element with a key of gilligan.crew.hut. Its initial value is undef, which acts like a zero when you add 1250 to it, and the result of 1250 is inserted back into the hash.

Any later data line that contains this same source host and destination host will reuse that same value, adding more bytes to the running total. But each new destination host extends a hash to include a new initially undef byte count, and each new source host uses autovivification to create a destination host hash. In other words, Perl does the right thing, as always.

Once you've processed the file, it's time to display the summary. First, you determine all the sources:

```
for my $source (keys %total_bytes) {
...
```

Now, you should get all destinations. The syntax for this is a bit tricky. You want all keys of the hash, resulting from dereferencing the value of the hash element, in the first structure:

```
for my $source (keys %total_bytes) {
  for my $destination (keys %{ $total_bytes{$source} }) {
....
```

For good measure, you should probably sort both lists to be consistent:

```
for my $source (sort keys %total_bytes) {
  for my $destination (sort keys %{ $total_bytes{$source} }) {
    print "$source => $destination:",
      " $total_bytes{$source}{$destination} bytes\n";
  }
  print "\n";
}
```

This is a typical data-reduction report generation strategy. Simply create a hash-of-hashrefs (perhaps nested even deeper, as you'll see later), using autovivification to fill in the gaps in the upper data structures as needed, and then walk through the resulting data structure to display the results.

Exercises

The answers for all exercises can be found in the Appendix.

Exercise 1 [5 min]

Without running it, can you see what's wrong with this piece of a program? If you can't see the problem after a minute or two, see whether trying to run it will give you a hint of how to fix it.

```
my %passenger_1 = {
  name => 'Ginger',
  age => 22,
  occupation => 'Movie Star',
  real_age => 35,
  hat => undef,
};

my %passenger_2 = {
  name => 'Mary Ann',
  age => 19,
  hat => 'bonnet',
  favorite_food => 'corn',
};

my @passengers = (\%passenger_1, \%passenger_2);
```

Exercise 2 [30 min]

The Professor's data file (mentioned earlier in this chapter) is available as coconet.dat in the files you can download from the O'Reilly web site. There may be comment lines (beginning with a pound sign); be sure to skip them. (That is, your program should skip them. You might find a helpful hint if *you* read them!)

Modify the code from the chapter so that each source machine's portion of the output shows the total number of bytes from that machine. List the source machines in order from most to least data transferred. Within each group, list the destination machines in order from most to least data transferred to that target from the source machine.

The result should be that the machine that sent the most data will be the first source machine in the list, and the first destination should be the machine to which it sent the most data. The Professor can use this printout to reconfigure the network for efficiency.

## CHAPTER 5

Manipulating Complex Data Structures

Now that you've seen the basics of references, let's look at additional ways to manipulate complex data. We'll start by using the debugger to examine complex data structures and then use Data::Dumper to show the data under programmatic control. Next, you'll learn to store and retrieve complex data easily and quickly using Storable, and finally we'll wrap up with a review of grep and map and see how they apply to complex data.

Using the Debugger to View Complex Data

The Perl debugger can display complex data easily. For example, let's single-step through one version of the byte-counting program from Chapter 4:

```
my %total_bytes;
while (<>) {
  my ($source, $destination, $bytes) = split;
  $total_bytes{$source}{$destination} += $bytes;
}
for my $source (sort keys %total_bytes) {
  for my $destination (sort keys %{ $total_bytes{$source} }) {
    print "$source => $destination:",
      " $total_bytes{$source}{$destination} bytes\n";
  }
  print "\n";
}
```

Here's the data you'll use to test it:

```
professor.hut gilligan.crew.hut 1250
professor.hut lovey.howell.hut 910
thurston.howell.hut lovey.howell.hut 1250
professor.hut lovey.howell.hut 450
ginger.girl.hut professor.hut 1218
ginger.girl.hut maryann.girl.hut 199
```

You can do this a number of ways. One of the easiest is to invoke Perl with a -d switch on the command line:

```
myhost% perl -d bytecounts bytecounts-in

Loading DB routines from perl5db.pl version 1.19
Editor support available.

Enter h or `h h' for help, or `man perldebug' for more help.

main::(bytecounts:2):        my %total_bytes;
  DB<1> s
main::(bytecounts:3):        while (<>) {
  DB<1> s
main::(bytecounts:4):          my ($source, $destination, $bytes) = split;
  DB<1> s
main::(bytecounts:5):            $total_bytes{$source}{$destination} += $bytes;
  DB<1> x $source, $destination, $bytes
0  'professor.hut'
1  'gilligan.crew.hut'
2  1250
```

If you're playing along at home, be aware that each new release of the debugger works differently than any other, so your screen probably won't look exactly like this. Also, if you get stuck at any time, type h for help, or look at perldoc perldebug.

Each line of code is shown before it is executed. That means that, at this point, you're about to invoke the autovivification, and you've got your keys established. The s command single-steps the program, while the x command dumps a list of values in a nice format. You can see that $source, $destination, and $bytes are correct, and now it's time to update the data:

```
  DB<2> s
main::(bytecounts:3):        while (<>) {
```

You've created the hash entries through autovivification. Let's see what you've got:

```
  DB<2> x \%total_bytes
0  HASH(0x132dc)
   'professor.hut' => HASH(0x37a34)
     'gilligan.crew.hut' => 1250
```

When x is given a hash reference, it dumps the entire contents of the hash, showing the key/value pairs. If any of the values are also hash references, they are dumped as well, recursively. What you'll see is that the %total_bytes hash has a single key of professor.hut, whose corresponding value is another hash reference. The referenced hash contains a single key of gilligan.crew.hut, with a value of 1250, as expected.

Let's see what happens just after the next assignment:

```
  DB<3> s
main::(bytecounts:4):          my ($source, $destination, $bytes) = split;
  DB<3> s
main::(bytecounts:5):            $total_bytes{$source}{$destination} += $bytes;
```

```
    DB<3> x $source, $destination, $bytes
0  'professor.hut'
1  'lovey.howell.hut'
2   910
    DB<4> s
main::(bytecounts:3):          while (<>) {
    DB<4> x \%total_bytes
0   HASH(0x132dc)
    'professor.hut' => HASH(0x37a34)
       'gilligan.crew.hut' => 1250
       'lovey.howell.hut' => 910
```

Now you've added bytes flowing from professor.hut to lovey.howell.hut. The top-level hash hasn't changed, but the second-level hash has added a new entry. Let's continue:

```
    DB<5> s
main::(bytecounts:4):          my ($source, $destination, $bytes) = split;
    DB<6> s
main::(bytecounts:5):          $total_bytes{$source}{$destination} += $bytes;
    DB<6> x $source, $destination, $bytes
0  'thurston.howell.hut'
1  'lovey.howell.hut'
2   1250
    DB<7> s
main::(bytecounts:3):          while (<>) {
    DB<7> x \%total_bytes
0   HASH(0x132dc)
    'professor.hut' => HASH(0x37a34)
       'gilligan.crew.hut' => 1250
       'lovey.howell.hut' => 910
    'thurston.howell.hut' => HASH(0x2f9538)
       'lovey.howell.hut' => 1250
```

Ah, now it's getting interesting. A new entry in the top-level hash has a key of thurston.howell.hut, and a new hash reference, autovivified initially to an empty hash. Immediately after the new empty hash was put in place, a new key/value pair was added, indicating 1250 bytes transferred from thurston.howell.hut to lovey.howell.hut. Let's step some more:

```
    DB<8> s
main::(bytecounts:4):          my ($source, $destination, $bytes) = split;
    DB<8> s
main::(bytecounts:5):          $total_bytes{$source}{$destination} += $bytes;
    DB<8> x $source, $destination, $bytes
0  'professor.hut'
1  'lovey.howell.hut'
2   450
    DB<9> s
main::(bytecounts:3):          while (<>) {
    DB<9> x \%total_bytes
0   HASH(0x132dc)
    'professor.hut' => HASH(0x37a34)
       'gilligan.crew.hut' => 1250
```

```
            'lovey.howell.hut' => 1360
    'thurston.howell.hut' => HASH(0x2f9538)
          'lovey.howell.hut' => 1250
```

Now you're adding in some more bytes from professor.hut to lovey.howell.hut, reusing the existing value place. Nothing too exciting there. Let's keep stepping:

```
    DB<10> s
main::(bytecounts:4):          my ($source, $destination, $bytes) = split;
    DB<10> s
main::(bytecounts:5):          $total_bytes{$source}{$destination} += $bytes;
    DB<10> x $source, $destination, $bytes
0   'ginger.girl.hut'
1   'professor.hut'
2   1218
    DB<11> s
main::(bytecounts:3):          while (<>) {
    DB<11> x \%total_bytes
0   HASH(0x132dc)
    'ginger.girl.hut' => HASH(0x297474)
        'professor.hut' => 1218
    'professor.hut' => HASH(0x37a34)
        'gilligan.crew.hut' => 1250
        'lovey.howell.hut' => 1360
    'thurston.howell.hut' => HASH(0x2f9538)
        'lovey.howell.hut' => 1250
```

This time, you added a new source, ginger.girl.hut. Notice that the top level hash now has three elements, and each element has a different hash reference value. Let's step some more:

```
    DB<12> s
main::(bytecounts:4):          my ($source, $destination, $bytes) = split;
    DB<12> s
main::(bytecounts:5):          $total_bytes{$source}{$destination} += $bytes;
    DB<12> x $source, $destination, $bytes
0   'ginger.girl.hut'
1   'maryann.girl.hut'
2   199
    DB<13> s
main::(bytecounts:3):          while (<>) {
    DB<13> x \%total_bytes
0   HASH(0x132dc)
    'ginger.girl.hut' => HASH(0x297474)
        'maryann.girl.hut' => 199
        'professor.hut' => 1218
    'professor.hut' => HASH(0x37a34)
        'gilligan.crew.hut' => 1250
        'lovey.howell.hut' => 1360
    'thurston.howell.hut' => HASH(0x2f9538)
        'lovey.howell.hut' => 1250
```

Now you've added a second destination to the hash that records information for all bytes originating at `ginger.girl.hut`. Because that was the final line of data (in this run), a step brings you down to the lower foreach loop:

```
DB<14> s
main::(bytecounts:8):          for my $source (sort keys %total_bytes) {
```

Even though you can't directly examine the list value from inside those parentheses, you can display it:

```
DB<14> x sort keys %total_bytes
0  'ginger.girl.hut'
1  'professor.hut'
2  'thurston.howell.hut'
```

This is the list the foreach now scans. These are all the sources for transferred bytes seen in this particular logfile. Here's what happens when you step into the inner loop:

```
DB<15> s
main::(bytecounts:9):          for my $destination (sort keys %{ $total bytes{
$source} }) {
```

At this point, you can determine from the inside out exactly what values will result from the list value from inside the parentheses. Let's look at them:

```
DB<15> x $source
0  'ginger.girl.hut'
DB<16> x $total_bytes{$source}
0  HASH(0x297474)
   'maryann.girl.hut' => 199
   'professor.hut' => 1218
DB<18> x keys %{ $total_bytes{$source } }
0  'maryann.girl.hut'
1  'professor.hut'
DB<19> x sort keys %{ $total_bytes{$source } }
0  'maryann.girl.hut'
1  'professor.hut'
```

Note that dumping `$total_bytes{$source}` shows that it was a hash reference. Also, the sort appears not to have done anything, but the output of keys is not necessarily in a sorted order. The next step finds the data:

```
DB<20> s
main::(bytecounts:10):         print "$source => $destination:",
main::(bytecounts:11):             " $total_bytes{$source}{$destination} bytes\n";
DB<20> x $source, $destination
0  'ginger.girl.hut'
1  'maryann.girl.hut'
DB<21> x $total_bytes{$source}{$destination}
0  199
```

As you can see, with the debugger, you can easily show the data, even structured data, to help you understand your program.

Viewing Complex Data with Data::Dumper

Another way to visualize a complex data structure rapidly is to *dump* it. A particularly nice dumping package is included in the Perl core distribution, called Data::Dumper. Let's replace the last half of the byte-counting program with a simple call to Data::Dumper:

```
use Data::Dumper;

my %total_bytes;
while (<>) {
  my ($source, $destination, $bytes) = split;
  $total_bytes{$source}{$destination} += $bytes;
}

print Dumper(\%total_bytes);
```

The Data::Dumper module defines the Dumper subroutine. This subroutine is similar to the x command in the debugger. You can give Dumper one or more values, and Dumper turns those values into a printable string. The difference between the debugger's x command and Dumper, however, is that the string generated by Dumper is Perl code:

```
myhost% perl bytecounts2 <bytecounts-in
$VAR1 = {
          'thurston.howell.hut' => {
                                     'lovey.howell.hut' => 1250
                                   },
          'ginger.girl.hut' => {
                                 'maryann.girl.hut' => 199,
                                 'professor.hut' => 1218
                               },
          'professor.hut' => {
                               'gilligan.crew.hut' => 1250,
                               'lovey.howell.hut' => 1360
                             }
        };
myhost%
```

The Perl code is fairly understandable; it shows that you have a reference to a hash of three elements, with each value of the hash being a reference to a nested hash. You can evaluate this code and get a hash that's equivalent to the original hash. However, if you're thinking about doing this in order to have a complex data structure persist from one program invocation to the next, please keep reading.

Data::Dumper, like the debugger's x command, handles shared data properly. For example, go back to that "leaking" data from Chapter 4:

```
use Data::Dumper;
$Data::Dumper::Purity = 1; # declare possibly self-referencing structures
my @data1 = qw(one won);
my @data2 = qw(two too to);
push @data2, \@data1;
```

```
push @data1, \@data2;
print Dumper(\@data1, \@data2);
```

Here's the output from this program:

```
$VAR1 = [
          'one',
          'won',
          [
            'two',
            'too',
            'to',
            []
          ]
        ];
$VAR1->[2][3] = $VAR1;
$VAR2 = $VAR1->[2];
```

Notice how you've created two different variables now, since there are two parameters to Dumper. The element $VAR1 corresponds to a reference to @data1, while $VAR2 corresponds to a reference to @data2. The debugger shows the values similarly:

```
DB<1> x \@data1, \@data2
    0  ARRAY(0xf914)
  0  'one'
  1  'won'
  2  ARRAY(0x3122a8)
    0  'two'
    1  'too'
    2  'to'
    3  ARRAY(0xf914)
       -> REUSED_ADDRESS
  1  ARRAY(0x3122a8)
  -> REUSED_ADDRESS
```

Note that the phrase REUSED_ADDRESS indicates that some parts of the data are actually references you've already seen.

Storing Complex Data with Storable

You can take the output of Data::Dumper's Dumper routine, place it into a file, and then load the file to a different program, evaluating the code as Perl code, and you'd end up with two package variables, $VAR1 and $VAR2, that are equivalent to the original data. This is called *marshaling* the data: converting complex data into a form that can be written to a file as a stream of bytes for later reconstruction.

However, another Perl core module is much better suited for marshaling: Storable. It's better suited because compared to Data::Dumper, Storable produces smaller and faster-to-process files. (The Storable module is standard in recent versions of Perl, but you can always install it from the CPAN if it's missing.)

The interface is similar to using Data::Dumper, except you must put everything into one reference. For example, let's store the mutually referencing data structures:

```
use Storable;
my @data1 = qw(one won);
my @data2 = qw(two too to);
push @data2, \@data1;
push @data1, \@data2;
store [\@data1, \@data2], 'some_file';
```

The file produced by this step was 68 bytes on this system, which was quite a bit shorter than the equivalent Data::Dumper output. It's also much less readable for humans. It's easy for Storable to read, as you'll soon see.[*]

Next, fetch the data, again using the Storable module. The result will be a single array reference. Dump the result to see if it stored the right values:

```
use Storable;
my $result = retrieve 'some_file';
use Data::Dumper;
$Data::Dumper::Purity = 1;
print Dumper($result);
```

Here's the result:

```
$VAR1 = [
          [
            'one',
            'won',
            [
              'two',
              'too',
              'to',
              []
            ]
          ],
          []
        ];
$VAR1->[0][2][3] = $VAR1->[0];
$VAR1->[1] = $VAR1->[0][2];
```

This is functionally the same as the original data structure. You're now looking at the two array references within one top-level array. To get something closer to what you saw before, you can be more explicit about the return value:

```
use Storable;
my ($arr1, $arr2) = @{ retrieve 'some_file' };
use Data::Dumper;
$Data::Dumper::Purity = 1;
print Dumper($arr1, $arr2);
```

---

[*] The format used by Storable is architecture byte-order dependent by default. The manpage shows how to create byte-order-independent storage files.

or equivalently:

```
use Storable;
my $result = retrieve 'some_file';
use Data::Dumper;
$Data::Dumper::Purity = 1;
print Dumper(@$result);
```

and you'll get:

```
$VAR1 = [
          'one',
          'won',
          [
            'two',
            'too',
            'to',
            []
          ]
        ];
$VAR1->[2][3] = $VAR1;
$VAR2 = $VAR1->[2];
```

just as you did in the original program. With Storable, you can store data and retrieve it later. More information on Storable can be found in perldoc Storable, as always.

The map and grep Operators

As the data structures become more complex, it helps to have higher-level constructs deal with common tasks such as selection and transformation. In this regard, Perl's grep and map operators are worth mastering.

Let's review the functionality of grep and map for a moment, without reference to references.

The grep operator takes a list of values and a "testing expression." For each item in the list of values, the item is placed temporarily into the $_ variable, and the testing expression is evaluated (in a scalar context). If the expression results in a true value (defined in the normal Perl sense of truth), the item is considered selected. In a list context, the grep operator returns a list of all such selected items. In a scalar context, the operator returns the number of selected items.[*]

The syntax comes in two forms: the expression form and the block form. The expression form is often easier to type:

```
my @results = grep $expression, @input_list;
my $count = grep $expression, @input_list;
```

---

[*] The value in $_ is local to the operation. If there's an existing $_ value, the local value temporarily shadows the global value while the grep executes.

Here, $expression is a scalar expression that should refer to $_ (explicitly or implic-itly). For example, find all the numbers greater than 10:

```
my @input_numbers = (1, 2, 4, 8, 16, 32, 64);
my @bigger_than_10 = grep $_ > 10, @input_numbers;
```

The result is just 16, 32, and 64. This uses an explicit reference to $_. Here's an example of an implicit reference to $_ that's similar to pattern matching:

```
my @end_in_4 = grep /4$/, @input_numbers;
```

And now you find just 4 and 64.

If the testing expression is complex, you can hide it in a subroutine:

```
my @odd_digit_sum = grep digit_sum_is_odd($_), @input_numbers;
sub digit_sum_is_odd {
  my $input = shift;
  my @digits = split //, $input;  # Assume no nondigit characters
  my $sum;
  $sum += $_ for @digits;
  return $sum % 2;
}
```

Now you get back the list of 1, 16, and 32. These numbers have a digit sum with a remainder of "1" in the last line of the subroutine, which counts as true.

However, rather than define an explicit subroutine used for only a single test, you can also put the body of a subroutine directly in line in the grep operator, using the block forms:*

```
my @results = grep { block; of; code; } @input_list;
my $count = grep { block; of; code; } @input_list;
```

Just like the expression form, each element of the input list is placed temporarily into $_. Next, the entire block of code is evaluated. The last expression evaluated in the block (evaluated in a scalar context) is used like the testing expression in the expres-sion form. Because it's a full block, you can introduce variables that are local to the block. Let's rewrite that last example to use the block form:

```
my @odd_digit_sum = grep {
  my $input = $_;
  my @digits = split //, $input;   # Assume no nondigit characters
  my $sum;
  $sum += $_ for @digits;
  $sum % 2;
} @input_numbers;
```

---

* In the block form of grep, there's no comma between the block and the input list. In the earlier (expression) form of grep, there must be a comma between the expression and the list.

Note the two changes: your input value comes in via $_ rather than an argument list, and the keyword return was removed. In fact, it would have been erroneous to retain the return because you're no longer in a separate subroutine: just a block of code.*

Of course, you can optimize a few things out of that routine:

```
my @odd_digit_sum = grep {
  my $sum;
  $sum += $_ for split //;
  $sum % 2;
} @input_numbers;
```

Feel free to crank up the explicitness if it helps you and your coworkers understand and maintain the code. That's the main thing that matters.

Using map

The map operator has a very similar syntax to the grep operator and shares a lot of the same operational steps. For example, items from a list of values are temporarily placed into $_ one at a time, and the syntax allows both a simple expression form and a more complex block form.

However, the testing expression becomes a mapping expression. This expression is evaluated in a list context (not a scalar context). Each evaluation of the expression gives a portion of the many results. The overall result is the list concatenation of all individual results. (In a scalar context, map returns the number of elements that are returned in a list context. But map should rarely, if ever, be used in anything but a list context.)

Let's start with a simple example:

```
my @input_numbers = (1, 2, 4, 8, 16, 32, 64);
my @result = map $_ + 100, @input_numbers;
```

For each of the seven items placed into $_, you get a single output result: the number that is 100 greater than the input number, so the value of @result is 101, 102, 104, 108, 116, 132, and 164.

But you're not limited to having only one output for each input. Let's see what happens when each input produces two output items:

```
my @result = map { $_, 3 * $_ } @input_numbers;
```

Now there are two items for each input item: 1, 3, 2, 6, 4, 12, 8, 24, 16, 48, 32, 96, 64, and 192. Those pairs can be stored in a hash, if you need a hash showing what number is three times a small power of two:

```
my %hash = @result;
```

---

* The return would have exited the subroutine that contains this entire section of code. And yes, some of us have been bitten by that mistake in real, live coding on the first draft.

Or, without using the intermediate array from the map:

```
my %hash = map { $_, 3 * $_ } @input_numbers;
```

You can see that map is pretty versatile; you can produce any number of output items for each input item. And you don't always need to produce the same number of output items. Let's see what happens when you break apart the digits:

```
my @result = map { split //, $_ } @input_numbers;
```

Each number is split into its digits. For 1, 2, 4, and 8, you get a single result. For 16, 32, and 64, you get two results per number. When the lists are concatenated, you end up with 1, 2, 4, 8, 1, 6, 3, 2, 6, and 4.

If a particular invocation results in an empty list, that empty result is concatenated into the larger list, contributing nothing to the list. You can use this feature to select and reject items. For example, suppose you want only the split digits of numbers ending in 4:

```
my @result = map {
  my @digits = split //, $_;
  if ($digits[-1] == 4) {
    @digits;
  } else {
    ();
  }
} @input_numbers;
```

If the last digit is 4, you return the digits themselves by evaluating @digits (which is evaluated in a list context). If the last digit is not 4, you return an empty list, effectively removing results for that particular item. (Thus, a map can always be used in place of a grep, but not vice versa.)

Of course, everything you can do with map and grep, you can also do with explicit foreach loops. But then again, you can also code in assembler or by toggling bits into a front panel.* The point is that proper application of grep and map can help reduce the complexity of the program, allowing you to concentrate on high-level issues rather than details.

Applying a Bit of Indirection

Some problems that may appear very complex are actually simple once you've seen a solution or two. For example, suppose you want to find the items in a list that have odd digit sums but don't want the items themselves. What you want to know is where they occurred in the original list.

---

* If you're old enough to remember those front panels.

All that's required is a bit of indirection.* First, you have a selection problem, so you use a grep. Let's not grep the values themselves but the index for each item:

```
my @input_numbers = (1, 2, 4, 8, 16, 32, 64);
my @indices_of_odd_digit_sums = grep {
  ...
} 0..$#input_numbers;
```

Here, the expression 0..$#input_numbers will be a list of indices for the array. Inside the block, $_ is a small integer, from 0 to 6 (seven items total). Now, you don't want to decide whether $_ has an odd digit sum. You want to know whether the array element at that index has an odd digit sum. Instead of using $_ to get the number of interest, use $input_numbers[$_]:

```
my @indices_of_odd_digit_sums = grep {
  my $number = $input_numbers[$_];
  my $sum;
  $sum += $_ for split //, $number;
  $sum % 2;
} 0..$#input_numbers;
```

The result will be the indices at which 1, 16, and 32 appear in the list: 0, 4, and 5. You could use these indices in an array slice to get the original values again:

```
my @odd_digit_sums = @input_numbers[ @indices_of_odd_digit_sums ];
```

The strategy here for an indirect grep or map is to think of the $_ values as identifying a particular item of interest, such as the key in a hash or the index of an array, and then use that identification within the block or expression to access the actual values.

Here's another example: select the elements of @x that are larger than the corresponding value in @y. Again, you'll use the indices of @x as your $_ items:

```
my @bigger_indices = grep {
  if ($_ > $#y or $x[$_] > $y[$_]) {
    1; # yes, select it
  } else {
    0; # no, don't select it
  }
} 0..$#x;
my @bigger = @x[@bigger_indices];
```

In the grep, $_ varies from 0 to the highest index of @x. If that element is beyond the end of @y, you automatically select it. Otherwise, you look at the individual corresponding values of the two arrays, selecting only the ones that meet your match.

However, this is a bit more verbose than it needs to be. You could simply return the boolean expression rather than a separate 1 or 0:

* A famous computing maxim states that "there is no problem so complex that it cannot be solved with appropriate additional layers of indirection." Of course, with indirection comes obfuscation, so there's got to be a magic middle ground somewhere.

```
my @bigger_indices = grep {
  $_ > $#y or $x[$_] > $y[$_];
} 0..$#x;
my @bigger = @x[@bigger_indices];
```

More easily, you can skip the step of building the intermediate array by simply
returning the items of interest with a map:

```
my @bigger = map {
  if ($_ > $#y or $x[$_] > $y[$_]) {
    $x[$_];
  } else {
    ();
  }
} 0..$#x;
```

If the index is good, return the resulting array value. If the index is bad, return an
empty list, making that item disappear.

Selecting and Altering Complex Data

You can use these operators on more complex data. Taking the provisions list from
Chapter 4:

```
my %provisions = (
  "The Skipper" =>
    [qw(blue_shirt hat jacket preserver sunscreen)],
  "The Professor" =>
    [qw(sunscreen water_bottle slide_rule batteries radio)],
  "Gilligan" =>
    [qw(red_shirt hat lucky_socks water_bottle)],
);
```

In this case, $provisions{"The Professor"} gives an array reference of the provisions
brought by the Professor, and $provisions{"Gilligan"}[-1] gives the last item Gilli-
gan thought to bring.

Run a few queries against this data. Who brought fewer than five items?

```
my @packed_light = grep @{ $provisions{$_} } < 5, keys %provisions;
```

In this case, $_ is the name of a person. Take that name, look up the array reference
of the provisions for that person, dereference that in a scalar context to get the count
of provisions, and then compare it to 5. And wouldn't you know it; the only name is
Gilligan.

Here's a trickier one. Who brought a water bottle?

```
my @all_wet = grep {
  my @items = @{ $provisions{$_} };
  grep $_ eq "water_bottle", @items;
} keys %provisions;
```

Starting with the list of names again (keys %provisions), pull up all the packed items first, and then use that list in an inner grep to count the number of those items that equal water_bottle. If the count is 0, there's no bottle, so the result is false for the outer grep. If the count is nonzero, you have a bottle, so the result is true for the outer grep. Now you see that the Skipper will be a bit thirsty later, without any relief.

You can also perform transformations. For example, turn this hash into a list of array references, with each array containing two items. The first is the original person's name; the second is a reference to an array of the provisions for that person:

```
my @remapped_list = map {
  [ $_ => $provisions{$_} ];
} keys %provisions;
```

The keys of %provisions are names of the people. For each name, construct a two-element list of the name and the corresponding provisions array reference. This list is inside an anonymous array constructor, so you get back a reference to a newly created array for each person. Three names in; three references out.[*]

Or, let's go a different way. Turn the input hash into a series of references to arrays. Each array will have a person's name and one of the items they brought:

```
my @person_item_pairs = map {
  my $person = $_;
  my @items = @{ $provisions{$person} };
  map [$person => $_], @items;
} keys %provisions;
```

Yes, a map within a map. The outer map selects one person at a time. The name is saved into $person, and then the item list is extracted from the hash. The inner map walks over this item list, executing the expression to construct an anonymous array reference for each item. The anonymous array contains the person's name and the provision item.

You had to use $person here to hold the outer $_ temporarily. Otherwise, you can't refer to both temporary values for the outer map and the inner map.

Exercises

The answers for all exercises can be found in the Appendix.

Exercise 1 [20 min]

The program from Exercise 2 in Chapter 4 needs to read the entire data file each time it runs. However, the Professor has a new router log file each day and doesn't want to keep all that data in one giant file that takes longer and longer to process.

---

[*] If you had left the inner brackets off, you'd end up with six items out. That's not very useful, unless you're creating a different hash from them.

Fix up that program to keep the running totals in a data file so the Professor can simply run it on each day's logs to get the new totals.

Exercise 2 [5 min]

To make it really useful, what other features should be added to that program? You don't need to implement them!

Subroutine References

So far, you've seen references to arrays and hashes. You can also take a reference to a *subroutine* (sometimes called a *coderef*).

Why would you want to do that? Well, in the same way that taking a reference to an array lets you have the same code work on different arrays at different times, taking a reference to a subroutine allows the same code to call different subroutines at different times. Also, references permit complex data structures. A reference to a subroutine allows a subroutine to effectively become part of that complex data structure.

Put another way, a variable or a complex data structure is a repository of values throughout the program. A reference to a subroutine can be thought of as a repository of *behavior* in a program. The examples in this section show how this works.

Referencing a Named Subroutine

The Skipper and Gilligan are having a conversation:

```
sub skipper_greets {
  my $person = shift;
  print "Skipper: Hey there, $person!\n";
}

sub gilligan_greets {
  my $person = shift;
  if ($person eq "Skipper") {
    print "Gilligan: Sir, yes, sir, $person!\n";
  } else {
    print "Gilligan: Hi, $person!\n";
  }
}

skipper_greets("Gilligan");
gilligan_greets("Skipper");
```

This results in:

```
Skipper: Hey there, Gilligan!
Gilligan: Sir, yes, sir, Skipper!
```

So far, nothing unusual has happened. Note however that Gilligan has two different behaviors, depending on whether he's addressing the Skipper or someone else.

Now, have the Professor walk into the hut. Both of the Minnow crew greet the newest participant:

```
skipper_greets("Professor");
gilligan_greets("Professor");
```

which results in

```
Skipper: Hey there, Professor!
Gilligan: Hi, Professor!
```

Now the Professor feels obligated to respond:

```
sub professor_greets {
  my $person = shift;
  print "Professor: By my calculations, you must be $person!\n";
}

professor_greets("Gilligan");
professor_greets("Skipper");
```

resulting in:

```
Professor: By my calculations, you must be Gilligan!\n";
Professor: By my calculations, you must be Skipper!\n";
```

Whew. A lot of typing and not very general. If each person's behavior is in a separate named subroutine and a new person walks in the door, you have to figure out what other subroutines to call. You could certainly do it with enough hard-to-maintain code, but you can simplify the process by adding a bit of indirection, just as you did with arrays and hashes.

First, let's introduce the "take a reference to" operator. It actually needs no introduction because it's that very same backslash again:

```
my $ref_to_greeter = \&skipper_greets;
```

You're taking a reference to the subroutine skipper_greets( ). Note that the preceding ampersand is mandatory here, and the lack of trailing parentheses is also intentional. The reference to the subroutine (a coderef) is stored within $ref_to_greeter, and like all other references, it fits nearly anywhere a scalar fits.

There's only one reason to get back to the original subroutine by dereferencing the coderef: to invoke it. Dereferencing a code reference is similar to dereferencing other references. First start with the way you would have written it before you heard of references (including the optional ampersand prefix):

```
& skipper_greets ( "Gilligan" )
```

Next, you replace the name of the subroutine with curly braces around the thing holding the reference:

```
& { $ref_to_greeter } ( "Gilligan" )
```

There you have it. This construct invokes the subroutine currently referenced by $ref_to_greeter, passing it the single Gilligan parameter.

But boy-oh-boy, is that ugly or what? Luckily, the same reference simplification rules apply. If the value inside the curly braces is a simple scalar variable, you can drop the braces:

```
& $ref_to_greeter ( "Gilligan" )
```

You can also flip it around a bit with the arrow notation:

```
$ref_to_greeter -> ( "Gilligan" )
```

That last form is particularly handy when the coderef is contained within a larger data structure, as you'll see in a moment.

To have both Gilligan and the Skipper greet the Professor, you merely need to iterate over all the subroutines:

```
for my $greet (\&skipper_greets, \&gilligan_greets) {
    $greet->("Professor");
}
```

First, inside the parentheses, you create a list of two items, each of which is a coderef. The coderefs are then individually dereferenced, invoking the corresponding subroutine and passing it the Professor string.

You've seen the coderefs in a scalar variable and as an element of a list. Can you put these coderefs into a larger data structure? Certainly. Create a table that maps people to the behavior they exhibit to greet others, and then rewrite that previous example using the table:

```
sub skipper_greets {
  my $person = shift;
  print "Skipper: Hey there, $person!\n";
}

sub gilligan_greets {
  my $person = shift;
  if ($person eq "Skipper") {
    print "Gilligan: Sir, yes, sir, $person!\n";
  } else {
    print "Gilligan: Hi, $person!\n";
  }
}

sub professor_greets {
  my $person = shift;
  print "Professor: By my calculations, you must be $person!\n";
}
```

```
my %greets = (
  "Gilligan" => \&gilligan_greets,
  "Skipper" => \&skipper_greets,
  "Professor" => \&professor_greets,
);

for my $person (qw(Skipper Gilligan)) {
  $greets{$person}->("Professor");
}
```

Note that $person is a name, which you look up in the hash to get to a coderef. Then you dereference that coderef, passing it the name of the person being greeted, and you get the correct behavior, resulting in:

```
Skipper: Hey there, Professor!
Gilligan: Hi, Professor!
```

Now have everyone greet everyone, in a very friendly room:

```
sub skipper_greets {
  my $person = shift;
  print "Skipper: Hey there, $person!\n";
}

sub gilligan_greets {
  my $person = shift;
  if ($person eq "Skipper") {
    print "Gilligan: Sir, yes, sir, $person!\n";
  } else {
    print "Gilligan: Hi, $person!\n";
  }
}

sub professor_greets {
  my $person = shift;
  print "Professor: By my calculations, you must be $person!\n";
}

my %greets = ... as before ...

my @everyone = sort keys %greets;
for my $greeter (@everyone) {
  for my $greeted (@everyone) {
    $greets{$greeter}->($greeted)
      unless $greeter eq $greeted; # no talking to yourself
  }
}
```

This results in:

```
Gilligan: Hi, Professor!
Gilligan: Sir, yes, sir, Skipper!
Professor: By my calculations, you must be Gilligan!
Professor: By my calculations, you must be Skipper!
Skipper: Hey there, Gilligan!
Skipper: Hey there, Professor!
```

Hmm. That's a bit complex. Let's let them walk into the room one at a time:

```
sub skipper_greets {
  my $person = shift;
  print "Skipper: Hey there, $person!\n";
}

sub gilligan_greets {
  my $person = shift;
  if ($person eq "Skipper") {
    print "Gilligan: Sir, yes, sir, $person!\n";
  } else {
    print "Gilligan: Hi, $person!\n";
  }
}

sub professor_greets {
  my $person = shift;
  print "Professor: By my calculations, you must be $person!\n";
}

my %greets = ... as before ...

my @room; # initially empty
for my $person (qw(Gilligan Skipper Professor)) {
  print "\n";
  print "$person walks into the room.\n";
  for my $room_person (@room) {
    $greets{$person}->($room_person); # speaks
    $greets{$room_person}->($person); # gets reply
  }
  push @room, $person; # come in, get comfy
}
```

The result is a typical day on that tropical island:

```
Gilligan walks into the room.

Skipper walks into the room.
Skipper: Hey there, Gilligan!
Gilligan: Sir, yes, sir, Skipper!

Professor walks into the room.
Professor: By my calculations, you must be Gilligan!
Gilligan: Hi, Professor!
Professor: By my calculations, you must be Skipper!
Skipper: Hey there, Professor!
```

Anonymous Subroutines

In that last example, subroutines such as professor_greets() were never called explicitly, but indirectly through the coderef. Thus, you wasted some brain cells to come up with a name for the subroutine used only in one other place, to initialize the data structure.

But as you can have anonymous hashes and arrays, you can have anonymous subroutines!

Let's add another island inhabitant: Ginger. But rather than define her greeting behavior as a named subroutine, create an anonymous subroutine:

```
my $ginger = sub {
  my $person = shift;
  print "Ginger: (in a sultry voice) Well hello, $person!\n";
};
$ginger->("Skipper");
```

An anonymous subroutine looks like:

```
sub { ... body of subroutine ... }
```

The value in $ginger is a coderef, just as if you had defined the following block as a subroutine and then taken a reference to it. When you reach the last statement, you see:

```
Ginger: (in a sultry voice) Well hello, Skipper!
```

Although you kept the value in a scalar variable, you could have put that sub { ... } construct directly into the initialization of the greetings hash:

```
my %greets = (

  "Skipper" => sub {
    my $person = shift;
    print "Skipper: Hey there, $person!\n";
  },

  "Gilligan" => sub {
    my $person = shift;
    if ($person eq "Skipper") {
      print "Gilligan: Sir, yes, sir, $person!\n";
    } else {
      print "Gilligan: Hi, $person!\n";
    }
  },

  "Professor" => sub {
    my $person = shift;
    print "Professor: By my calculations, you must be $person!\n";
  },

  "Ginger" => sub {
    my $person = shift;
    print "Ginger: (in a sultry voice) Well hello, $person!\n";
  },

);
```

```
my @room; # initially empty
for my $person (qw(Gilligan Skipper Professor Ginger)) {
  print "\n";
  print "$person walks into the room.\n";
  for my $room_person (@room) {
    $greets{$person}->($room_person); # speaks
    $greets{$room_person}->($person); # gets reply
  }
  push @room, $person; # come in, get comfy
}
```

Notice how much it simplifies the code. The subroutine definitions are right within the only data structure that references them directly. The result is straightforward:

```
Gilligan walks into the room.

Skipper walks into the room.
Skipper: Hey there, Gilligan!
Gilligan: Sir, yes, sir, Skipper!

Professor walks into the room.
Professor: By my calculations, you must be Gilligan!
Gilligan: Hi, Professor!
Professor: By my calculations, you must be Skipper!
Skipper: Hey there, Professor!

Ginger walks into the room.
Ginger: (in a sultry voice) Well hello, Gilligan!
Gilligan: Hi, Ginger!
Ginger: (in a sultry voice) Well hello, Skipper!
Skipper: Hey there, Ginger!
Ginger: (in a sultry voice) Well hello, Professor!
Professor: By my calculations, you must be Ginger!
```

Adding a few more castaways is as simple as putting the entry for the greeting behavior into the hash and adding them into the list of people entering the room. You get this scaling of effort because you've preserved the behavior as data over which you can iterate and look up, thanks to your friendly subroutine references.

Callbacks

A subroutine reference is often used for a *callback*. A callback defines what to do when a subroutine reaches a particular place in an algorithm.

For example, the File::Find module exports a find subroutine that can efficiently walk through a given filesystem hierarchy in a fairly portable way. In its simplest form, you give the find subroutine two parameters: a starting directory and "what to do" for each file or directory name found recursively below that starting directory. The "what to do" is specified as a subroutine reference:

```
use File::Find;
sub what_to_do {
```

```
      print "$File::Find::name found\n";
    }
    my @starting_directories = qw(.);

    find(\&what_to_do, @starting_directories);
```

In this case, find starts at the current directory (.) and locates each file or directory. For each item, a call is made to the subroutine what_to_do( ), passing it a few documented values through global variables. In particular, the value of $File::Find::name is the item's full pathname (beginning with the starting directory).

In this case, you're passing both data (the list of starting directories) and *behavior* as parameters to the find routine.

It's a bit silly to invent a subroutine name just to use the name only once, so you can write the previous code using an anonymous subroutine, such as:

```
    use File::Find;
    my @starting_directories = qw(.);

    find(
      sub {
        print "$File::Find::name found\n";
      },
      @starting_directories,
    );
```

Closures

You could also use File::Find to find out some other things about files, such as their size. For the callback's convenience, the current working directory is the item's containing directory, and the item's name within that directory is found in $_.

Maybe you have noticed that, in the previous code, $File::Find::name was used for the item's name. So which name is real, $_ or $File::Find::name?

$File::Find::name gives the name relative to the starting directory, but during the callback, the working directory is the one that holds the item just found. For example, suppose that you want find to look for files in the current working directory, so you give it (".") as the list of directories to search. If you call find when the current working directory is /usr, find looks below that directory. When find has located /usr/bin/perl, the current working directory (during the callback) is /usr/bin. $_ holds "perl"; $File::Find::name holds "./bin/perl", which is the name relative to the directory in which you started the search.

All of this means that the file tests, such as -s, automatically report on the just-found item. Although this is convenient, the current directory inside the callback is different from the search's starting directory.

What if you want to use `File::Find` to accumulate the total size of all files seen? The callback subroutine doesn't support either parameters to be passed in, nor a result returned from the subroutine. But that doesn't matter. When dereferenced, a subroutine reference can "see" all visible lexical variables when the reference to the subroutine is taken. For example:

```
use File::Find;

my $total_size = 0;
find(sub { $total_size += -s if -f }, ".");
print $total_size, "\n";
```

As before, the `find` routine is called with two parameters: a reference to an anonymous subroutine and the starting directory. When names are found within that directory (and its subdirectories), the subroutine is called.

Note that the subroutine accesses the `$total_size` variable. This variable is declared outside the scope of the subroutine but still visible to the subroutine. Thus, even though `find` invokes the callback subroutine (and would not have direct access to `$total_size`), the callback subroutine accesses and updates the variable.

The kind of subroutine that can access all lexical variables that existed at the time it was declared is called a *closure* (a term borrowed from the world of mathematics).

Furthermore, the access to the variable from within the closure ensures that the variable remains alive as long as the subroutine reference is alive. For example, let's number the output files:*

```
use File::Find;

my $callback;
{
  my $count = 0;
  $callback = sub { print ++$count, ": $File::Find::name\n" };
}
find($callback, ".");
```

Here, you declare a variable to hold the callback. This variable cannot be declared within the naked block (the block following that is not part of a larger Perl syntax construct), or it would be recycled at the end of that block. Next, the lexical `$count` variable is initialized to 0. An anonymous subroutine is then declared, and a reference to it is placed into `$callback`. This subroutine is a closure because it refers to the lexical `$count` variable.

---

* This code seems to have an extra semicolon at the end of the line that assigns to `$callback`, doesn't it? But remember, the construct `sub { ... }` is an expression. Its value (a coderef) is assigned to `$callback`, and there's a semicolon at the end of that statement. It's easy to forget to put the proper punctuation after the closing curly brace of an anonymous subroutine declaration.

At the end of the naked block, the $count variable goes out of scope. However, because it is still referenced by subroutine in $callback, it stays alive, now as an anonymous scalar variable.*

When the callback is invoked from find, the value of the variable formerly known as $count is incremented from 1 to 2 to 3, and so on.

Returning a Subroutine from a Subroutine

Although a naked block worked nicely to define the callback, having a subroutine return that subroutine reference instead might be more useful:

```
use File::Find;

sub create_find_callback_that_counts {
  my $count = 0;
  return sub { print ++$count, ": $File::Find::name\n" };
}

my $callback = create_find_callback_that_counts();
find($callback, ".");
```

It's the same process here, just written a bit differently. When you invoke create_find_callback_that_counts( ), a lexical variable $count is initialized to 0. The return value from that subroutine is a reference to an anonymous subroutine that is also a closure because it accesses the $count variable. Even though $count goes out of scope at the end of the create_find_callback_that_counts( ) subroutine, there's still a binding between it and the returned subroutine reference, so the variable stays alive until the subroutine reference is finally discarded.

If you reuse the callback, the same variable still has its most recently used value. The initialization occurred in the original subroutine (create_find_callback_that_counts), not the callback (unnamed) subroutine:

```
use File::Find;

sub create_find_callback_that_counts {
  my $count = 0;
  return sub { print ++$count, ": $File::Find::name\n" };
}

my $callback = create_find_callback_that_counts();
print "my bin:\n";
find($callback, "bin");
print "my lib:\n";
find($callback, "lib");
```

---

* To be more accurate, the closure declaration increases the reference count of the referent, as if another reference had been taken explicitly. Just before the end of the naked block, the reference count of $count is two, but after the block has exited, the value still has a reference count of one. Although no other code may access $count, it will still be kept in memory as long as the reference to the sub is available in $callback or elsewhere.

This example prints consecutive numbers starting at 1 for the entries below my bin, but then continues the numbering when you start entries in lib. The same $count variable is used in both cases. However, if you invoke the create_find_callback_that_counts( ) twice, you get two different $count variables:

```
use File::Find;

sub create_find_callback_that_counts {
  my $count = 0;
  return sub { print ++$count, ": $File::Find::name\n" };
}

my $callback1 = create_find_callback_that_counts( );
my $callback2 = create_find_callback_that_counts( );
print "my bin:\n";
find($callback1, "bin");
print "my lib:\n";
find($callback2, "lib");
```

In this case, you have two separate $count variables, each accessed from within their own callback subroutine.

How would you get the total size of all found files from the callback? Earlier, you were able to do this by making $total_size visible. If you stick the definition of $total_size into the subroutine that returns the callback reference, you won't have access to the variable. But you can cheat a bit. For one thing, you can determine that the callback subroutine is never called with any parameters, so, if the subroutine is called with a parameter, you can make it return the total size:

```
use File::Find;

sub create_find_callback_that_sums_the_size {
  my $total_size = 0;
  return sub {
    if (@_) { # it's our dummy invocation
      return $total_size;
    } else { # it's a callback from File::Find:
      $total_size += -s if -f;
    }
  };
}

my $callback = create_find_callback_that_sums_the_size( );
find($callback, "bin");
my $total_size = $callback->("dummy"); # dummy parameter to get size
print "total size of bin is $total_size\n";
```

Distinguishing actions by the presence or absence of parameters is not a universal solution. Fortunately, more than one subroutine reference can be created in create_find_callback_that_counts( ):

```
use File::Find;

sub create_find_callbacks_that_sum_the_size {
```

```
   my $total_size = 0;
   return(sub { $total_size += -s if -f }, sub { return $total_size });
}

my ($count_em, $get_results) = create_find_callbacks_that_sum_the_size();
find($count_em, "bin");
my $total_size = &$get_results();
print "total size of bin is $total_size\n";
```

Because both subroutine references were created from the same scope, they both have access to the same $total_size variable. Even though the variable has gone out of scope before either subroutine is called, they still share the same heritage and can use the variable to communicate the result of the calculation.

The two subroutine references are not invoked by returning their references from the creating subroutine. The references are just data at that point. It's not until you invoke them as a callback or an explicit subroutine derefencing that they actually do their duty.

What if you invoke this new subroutine more than once?

```
use File::Find;

sub create_find_callbacks_that_sum_the_size {
  my $total_size = 0;
  return(sub { $total_size += -s if -f }, sub { return $total_size });
}

## set up the subroutines
my %subs;
foreach my $dir (qw(bin lib man)) {
  my ($callback, $getter) = create_find_callbacks_that_sum_the_size();
  $subs{$dir}{CALLBACK} = $callback;
  $subs{$dir}{GETTER} = $getter;
}

## gather the data
for (keys %subs) {
  find($subs{$_}{CALLBACK}, $_);
}

## show the data
for (sort keys %subs) {
  my $sum = $subs{$_}{GETTER}->();
  print "$_ has $sum bytes\n";
}
```

In the "set up the subroutines" section, you create three instances of callback-and-getter pairs. Each callback has a corresponding subroutine to get the results. Next, in the "gather the data" section, you call find three times with each corresponding callback subroutine reference. This updates the individual $total_size variables associated with each callback. Finally, in the "show the data" section, you call the getter routines to fetch the results.

The six subroutines (and the three $total_size variables they share) are reference-counted. When %subs goes away or is modified, the values have their reference counts reduced, recycling the contained data. (If that data also references further data, those reference counts are also reduced appropriately.)

Closure Variables as Inputs

While the previous examples showed closure variables being modified, closure variables are also useful to provide initial or lasting input to the subroutine. For example, let's write a subroutine to create a File::Find callback that prints files exceeding a certain size:

```
use File::Find;

sub print_bigger_than {
  my $minimum_size = shift;
  return sub { print "$File::Find::name\n" if -f and -s >= $minimum_size };
}

my $bigger_than_1024 = print_bigger_than(1024);
find($bigger_than_1024, "bin");
```

The 1024 parameter is passed into the print_bigger_than, which then gets shifted into the $minimum_size lexical variable. Because you access this variable within the subroutine referenced by the return value of the print_bigger_than variable, it becomes a closure variable, with a value that persists for the duration of that subroutine reference. Again, invoking this subroutine multiple times creates distinct "locked-in" values for $minimum_size, each bound to its corresponding subroutine reference.

Closures are "closed" only on lexical variables, since lexical variables eventually go out of scope. Because a package variable (which is a global) never goes out of scope, a closure never closes on a package variable. All subroutines refer to the same single instance of the global variable.

Closure Variables as Static Local Variables

A subroutine doesn't have to be an anonymous subroutine to be a closure. If a named subroutine accesses lexical variables and those variables go out of scope, the named subroutine retains a reference to the lexicals, just as you saw with anonymous subroutines. For example, consider two routines that count coconuts for Gilligan:

```
{
  my $count;
  sub count_one { ++$count }
```

```
    sub count_so_far { return $count }
}
```

If you place this code at the beginning of the program, the variable $count is declared, and the two subroutines that reference the variable become closures. However, because they have a name, they will persist beyond the end of the scope (as do all named subroutines). Since the subroutines persist beyond the scope and access variables declared within that scope, they become closures and thus can continue to access $count throughout the lifetime of the program.

So, with a few calls, you can see an incremented count:

```
count_one( );
count_one( );
count_one( );
print "we have seen ", count_so_far( ), " coconuts!\n";
```

$count retains its value between calls to count_one( ) or count_so_far( ), but no other section of code can access this $count at all.

In C, this is known as a *static local* variable: a variable that is visible to only a subset of the program's subroutines but persists throughout the life of the program, even between calls to those subroutines.

What if you wanted to count down? Something like this will do:

```
{
    my $countdown = 10;
    sub count_down { $countdown-- }
    sub count_remaining { $countdown }
}

count_down( );
count_down( );
count_down( );
print "we're down to ", count_remaining( ), " coconuts!\n";
```

That is, it'll do as long as you put it near the beginning of the program, before any invocations of count_down( ) or count_remaining( ). Why?

This block doesn't work when you put it after those invocations because there are two functional parts to the first line:

```
my $countdown = 10;
```

One part is the declaration of $countdown as a lexical variable. That part is noticed and processed as the program is parsed during the *compile phase*. The second part is the assignment of 10 to the allocated storage. This is handled as the code is executed during the *run phase*. Unless the run phase is executed for this code, the variable has its initial undef value.

One practical solution to this problem is to change the block in which the static local appears into a BEGIN block:

```
BEGIN {
  my $countdown = 10;
  sub count_down { $countdown-- }
  sub count_remaining { $countdown }
}
```

The BEGIN keyword tells the Perl compiler that as soon as this block has been parsed successfully (during the compile phase), jump for a moment to run phase and run the block as well. Presuming the block doesn't cause a fatal error, compilation then continues with the text following the block. The block itself is also discarded, ensuring that the code within is executed precisely once in a program, even if it had appeared syntactically within a loop or subroutine.

Exercise

The answers for all exercises can be found in the Appendix.

Exercise [30 min]

The Professor modified some files on Monday afternoon, and now he's forgotten which ones they were. This happens all the time. He wants you to make a subroutine called gather_mtime_between, which, given a starting and ending timestamp, returns a pair of coderefs. The first one will be used with File::Find to gather the names of only the items that were modified between those two times; the second one should return the list of items found.

Here's some code to try; it should list only items that were last modified on the most recent Monday, although you could easily change it to work with a different day. (You don't have to type all of this code. This program should be available as the file named ex6-1.plx in the downloadable files, available on the O'Reilly web site.)

Hint: You can find a file's timestamp (mtime) with code such as:

```
my $timestamp = (stat $file_name)[9];
```

Because it's a slice, remember that those parentheses are mandatory. Don't forget that the working directory inside the callback isn't necessarily the starting directory in which find was called.

```
use File::Find;
use Time::Local;

my $target_dow = 1;        # Sunday is 0, Monday is 1, ...
my @starting_directories = (".");

my $seconds_per_day = 24 * 60 * 60;
my($sec, $min, $hour, $day, $mon, $yr, $dow) = localtime;
my $start = timelocal(0, 0, 0, $day, $mon, $yr);        # midnight today
while ($dow != $target_dow) {
  # Back up one day
```

```perl
    $start -= $seconds_per_day;          # hope no DST! :-)
    if (--$dow < 0) {
      $dow += 7;
    }
  }
}
my $stop = $start + $seconds_per_day;

my($gather, $yield)  = gather_mtime_between($start, $stop);
find($gather, @starting_directories);
my @files = $yield->( );

for my $file (@files) {
  my $mtime = (stat $file)[9];          # mtime via slice
  my $when = localtime $mtime;
  print "$when: $file\n";
}
```

Note the comment about DST. In many parts of the world, on the days when daylight savings time or summer time kicks in and out, the day is no longer 86,400 seconds long. The program glosses over this issue, but a more pedantic coder might take it into consideration appropriately.

## CHAPTER 7

Practical Reference Tricks

This chapter looks at optimizing sorting and dealing with recursively defined data.

Review of Sorting

Perl's built-in sort operator sorts text strings in their natural text order, by default.[*] This is fine if you want to sort text strings:

```
my @sorted = sort qw(Gilligan Skipper Professor Ginger Mary_Ann);
```

but gets pretty messy when you want to sort numbers:

```
my @wrongly_sorted = sort 1, 2, 4, 8, 16, 32;
```

The resulting list is 1, 16, 2, 32, 4, 8. Why didn't sort order these properly? It treats each item as a string and sorts them in string order. Any string that begins with 3 sorts before any string that begins with 4.

You can fix this by overriding how Perl compares pairs of items in the list. By default, as Perl orders the items, a string comparison is used. A new comparison is specified using a *sort block*, placed between the sort keyword and the list of things to sort.[†]

Within the sort block, $a and $b stand in for two of the items to be sorted. The last evaluated expression must return a -1, 0, or +1 value.[‡] If the value is -1, the value currently in $a must appear before the value in $b in the final sorted list. If the value is

---

[*] My friends call that the "ASCIIbetical" ordering. Normally modern Perl doesn't use ASCII; instead, it uses a default sort order, depending on the current locale and character set; see the perllocale (not perllocal!) manpage.

[†] A sort block can also be specified as a subroutine name, causing the subroutine to be invoked when a comparison is needed.

[‡] Actually, you can use any negative or positive number in place of -1 and +1, respectively.

+1, then the value in $a must appear after the value in $b in the final sorted list. If the value is 0, you don't know or can't tell, so the results are unpredictable.[*]

For example, to sort those numbers in their proper order, you can use a sort block comparing $a and $b, like so:

```
my @numerically_sorted = sort {
  if ($a < $b)     { -1 }
  elsif ($a > $b) { +1 }
  else            {  0 }
} 1, 2, 4, 8, 16, 32;
```

Now you have a proper numeric comparison, so you have a proper numeric sort. Of course, this is far too much typing, so you can use the spaceship operator instead:

```
my @numerically_sorted = sort { $a <=> $b } 1, 2, 4, 8, 16, 32;
```

The spaceship operator returns -1, 0, and +1, according to the rules discussed. A descending sort is as simple as reversing the position of $a and $b:

```
my @numerically_descending = sort { $b <=> $a } 1, 2, 4, 8, 16, 32;
```

In every place the previous sort expression returned -1, this expression returns +1, and vice versa. Thus, the sort is in the opposite order. It's also easy to remember because if $a is to the left of $b, you get out the lower items first, just like a and b would be in the resulting list.

Likewise, a string sort can be indicated with cmp, although this is used less often because it is the default comparison. The cmp operator is handier when you have a more complex comparison, as you'll see shortly.

Sorting with Indices

In the same way you used indices to solve a few problems with grep and map back in Chapter 5, you can also use indices with sort to get some interesting results. For example, let's sort the list of names from earlier:

```
my @sorted = sort qw(Gilligan Skipper Professor Ginger Mary_Ann);
print "@sorted\n";
```

which necessarily results in:

```
Gilligan Ginger Mary_Ann Professor Skipper
```

But what if you wanted to look at the original list and determine which element of the original list now appears as the first, second, third, and so on, element of the sorted list? For example, Ginger is the second element of the sorted list and was the

---

[*] Recent Perl versions include a default sorting engine that is *stable*, so zero returns from the sort block cause the relative ordering of $a and $b to reflect their order in the original list. Older versions of Perl didn't guarantee such stability, and a future version might not use a stable sort, so don't rely on it.

fourth element of the original list. How do you determine that the second element of the final list was the fourth element of the original list?

Well, you can apply a bit of indirection. Let's not sort the actual names but rather the indices of each name:

```
my @input = qw(Gilligan Skipper Professor Ginger Mary_Ann);
my @sorted_positions = sort { $input[$a] cmp $input[$b] } 0..$#input;
print "@sorted_positions\n";
```

This prints 0 3 4 2 1, which means that the first element of the sorted list is element 0 of the original list, Gilligan. The second element of the sorted list is element 3 of the original list, which is Ginger, and so on. Now you can rank information rather than just move the names around.

Actually, you have the inverse of the rank. You still don't know for a given name in the original list about which position it occupies in the output list. But with a bit more magic, you can get there as well:

```
my @input = qw(Gilligan Skipper Professor Ginger Mary_Ann);
my @sorted_positions = sort { $input[$a] cmp $input[$b] } 0..$#input;
my @ranks;
@ranks[@sorted_positions] = (0..$#sorted_positions);
print "@ranks\n";
```

The code prints 0 4 3 1 2. This means that Gilligan is position 0 in the output list, Skipper is position 4, Professor is position 2, and so on. The positions here are 0-based, so add 1 to get "human" ordinal values. One way to cheat is to use 1..@sorted_positions instead of 0..$#sorted_positions, so a way to dump it all out might look like:

```
my @input = qw(Gilligan Skipper Professor Ginger Mary_Ann);
my @sorted_positions = sort { $input[$a] cmp $input[$b] } 0..$#input;
my @ranks;
@ranks[@sorted_positions] = (1..@sorted_positions);
for (0..$#ranks) {
  print "$input[$_] sorts into position $ranks[$_]\n";
}
```

This results in:

```
Gilligan sorts into position 1
Skipper sorts into position 5
Professor sorts into position 4
Ginger sorts into position 2
Mary_Ann sorts into position 3
```

Sorting Efficiently

As the Professor tries to maintain the community computing facility (built entirely out of bamboo, coconuts, and pineapples, and powered by a live monkey), he continues to discover that people are leaving entirely too much data on the single monkey-powered filesystem and decides to print a list of offenders.

The Professor has written a subroutine called ask_monkey_about( ) which is given a castaway's name and returns the number of pineapples of storage they use. You have to ask the monkey because he's in charge of the pineapples. An initial naive approach to find the offenders from greatest to least might be something like:

```
my @castaways =
  qw(Gilligan Skipper Professor Ginger Mary_Ann Thurston Lovey);
my @wasters = sort {
  ask_monkey_about($b) <=> ask_monkey_about($a)
} @castaways;
```

In theory, this would be fine. For the first pair of names (Gilligan and Skipper), you ask the monkey "how many pineapples does Gilligan have?" and "how many pineapples does Skipper have?" You get back two values from the monkey and use them to order Gilligan and Skipper in the final list.

However, at some point, you have to compare the number of pineapples that Gilligan has with another castaway as well. For example, suppose the pair is Ginger and Gilligan. Ask the monkey about Ginger, get a number back, and then ask the monkey about Gilligan...again. This will probably annoy the monkey a bit, since you already asked earlier. But you need to ask for each value two, three, or maybe even four times just to put the seven values into order.

This can be a problem because it irritates the monkey.

How do you keep the number of monkey requests to a minimum? Well, you can build a table first. Use a map with seven inputs and seven outputs, turning each castaway item into a separate array reference, with each referenced array consisting of the castaway name and the pineapple count reported by the monkey:

```
my @names_and_pineapples = map {
  [ $_, ask_monkey_about($_) ]
} @castaways;
```

At this point, you asked the monkey seven questions in a row, but that's the last time you have to talk to the monkey! You now have everything you need to finish the task.

For the next step, sort the arrayrefs, ordering them by the monkey-returned value:

```
my @sorted_names_and_pineapples = sort {
  $b->[1] <=> $a->[1];
} @names_and_pineapples;
```

In this subroutine, $a and $b are still two elements from the list of things to be sorted. When you're sorting numbers, $a and $b are numbers; when you're sorting references, $a and $b are references. Dereference them to get to the corresponding array itself, and pick out item 1 from the array (the monkey's pineapple value). Because $b appears to the left of $a, it'll be a descending sort as well. (You want a descending sort because the Professor wants the first name on the list to be the person who uses the most pineapples.)

You're almost done, but what if you just wanted the top names, rather than the names and pineapple counts? You merely need to perform another map to transform the references back to the original data:

```
my @names = map $_->[0], @sorted_names_and_pineapples;
```

Each element of the list ends up in $_, so you'll dereference that to pick out the element 0 of that array, which is just the name.

Now you have a list of names, ordered by their pineapple counts, and a calm monkey, all in three easy steps.

The Schwartzian Transform

The intermediate variables between each of these steps were not necessary, except as input to the next step. You can save yourself some brainpower by just stacking all the steps together:

```
my @names =
  map $_->[0],
  sort { $b->[1] <=> $a->[1] }
  map [ $_, ask_monkey_about($_) ],
  @castaways;
```

Because the map and sort operators are right to left, you have to read this construct from the bottom up. Take a list of @castaways, create some arrayrefs by asking the monkey a simple question, sort the list of arrayrefs, and then extract the names from each arrayref. This gives you the list of names in the desired order.

This construct is commonly called the *Schwartzian Transform*, which was named after me (but not by me), thanks to a Usenet posting I made many years ago. It has proven to be a very nice thing to have in your bag of sorting tricks.

If this transform looks like it might be too complex to memorize or come up with from first principles, it might help to look at the flexible and constant parts:

```
my @output_data =
  map $_->[0],
  sort { SORT COMPARISON USING $a->[1] AND $b->[1] }
  map [ $_, EXPENSIVE FUNCTION OF $_ ],
  @input_data;
```

The basic structure maps the original list into a list of arrayrefs, computing the expensive function only once for each; sorts those array refs, looking at the cached value of each expensive function invocation;* and then extracts the original values

---

* An *expensive* operation is one that takes a relatively long time or a relatively large amount of memory.

back out in the new order. All you have to do is plug in the proper two operations, and you're done.

Recursively Defined Data

While the data you've processed with references up to this point has been rather fixed-structure, sometimes you have to deal with hierarchical data, which is often defined recursively.

For example, a company organization chart has managers with direct reports, some of whom may also be managers themselves, or an HTML table that has rows containing cells—and some of those cells may also contain entire tables. The chart could also show a filesystem consisting of directories containing files and other directories.

You can use references to acquire, store, and process such hierarchical information. Frequently, the routines to manage the data structures end up as recursive subroutines. A recursive subroutine has a branch from which it calls itself to handle a portion of the task, and a branch that doesn't call itself to handle the base cases.

For example, a recursive subroutine handling the factorial function, which is one of the simplest recursive functions, might look like:

```
sub factorial {
  my $n = shift;
  if ($n <= 1) {
    return 1;
  } else {
    return $n * factorial($n - 1);
  }
}
```

Here you have a base case where $n is less than or equal to 1, that does not invoke the recursive instance, along with a recursive case for $n greater than 1, which calls the routine to handle a portion of the problem (i.e., compute the factorial of the next lower number).

This task would probably be solved better using iteration rather than recursion, even though the classic definition of factorial is often given as a recursive operation.

Building Recursively Defined Data

Suppose you wanted to capture information about a filesystem, including the filenames and directory names, and their included contents. Represent a directory as a hash, in which the keys are the names of the entries within the directory, and values are undef for plain files. A sample /bin directory might look like:

```
my $bin_directory = {
  "cat" => undef,
  "cp" => undef,
```

```
    "date" => undef,
    ... and so on ...
};
```

Similarly, the Skipper's home directory might also contain a personal bin directory (at something like ~skipper/bin) that contains personal tools:

```
my $skipper_bin = {
  "navigate" => undef,
  "discipline_gilligan" => undef,
  "eat" => undef,
};
```

nothing in either structure tells where the directory is located in the hierarchy. It just represents the contents of some directory.

Go up one level to the Skipper's home directory, which is likely to contain a few files along with the personal bin directory:

```
my $skipper_home = {
  ".cshrc" => undef,
  "Please_rescue_us.pdf" => undef,
  "Things_I_should_have_packed" => undef,
  "bin" => $skipper_bin,
};
```

Ahh, notice that you have three files, but the fourth entry "bin" doesn't have undef for a value but rather the hash reference created earlier for the Skipper's personal bin directory. This is how you indicate subdirectories. If the value is undef, it's a plain file; if it's a hash reference, you have a subdirectory, with its own files and subdirectories. Of course, you can have combined these two initializations:

```
my $skipper_home = {
  ".cshrc" => undef,
  "Please_rescue_us.pdf" => undef,
  "Things_I_should_have_packed" => undef,
  "bin" => {
    "navigate" => undef,
    "discipline_gilligan" => undef,
    "eat" => undef,
  },
};
```

Now the hierarchical nature of the data starts to come into play.

Obviously, you don't want to create and maintain a data structure by changing literals in the program. You should fetch the data by using a subroutine. Write a subroutine that for a given pathname returns undef if the path is a file, or a hash reference of the directory contents if the path is a directory. The base case of looking at a file is the easiest, so let's write that:

```
sub data_for_path {
  my $path = shift;
  if (-f $path) {
    return undef;
```

```
    }
    if (-d $path) {
        ...
    }
    warn "$path is neither a file nor a directory\n";
    return undef;
}
```

If the Skipper calls this on .cshrc, he'll get back an undef value, indicating that a file was seen.

Now for the directory part. You need a hash reference to be returned, which you declare as a named hash inside the subroutine. For each element of the hash, you call yourself to populate the value of that hash element. It goes something like this:

```
sub data_for_path {
    my $path = shift;
    if (-f $path or -l $path) {        # files or symbolic links
        return undef;
    }
    if (-d $path) {
        my %directory;
        opendir PATH, $path or die "Cannot opendir $path: $!";
        my @names = readdir PATH;
        closedir PATH;
        for my $name (@names) {
            next if $name eq "." or $name eq "..";
            $directory{$name} = data_for_path("$path/$name");
        }
        return \%directory;
    }
    warn "$path is neither a file nor a directory\n";
    return undef;
}
```

For each file within the directory being examined, the response from the recursive call to data_for_path is undef. This populates most elements of the hash. When the reference to the named hash is returned, the reference becomes a reference to an anonymous hash because the name immediately goes out of scope. (The data itself doesn't change, but the number of ways in which you can access the data changes.)

If there is a subdirectory, the nested subroutine call uses readdir to extract the contents of that directory and returns a hash reference, which is inserted into the hash structure created by the caller.

At first, it may look a bit mystifying, but if you walk through the code slowly, you'll see it's always doing the right thing.

Test the results of this subroutine by calling it on . (the current directory) and seeing the result:

```
use Data::Dumper;
print Dumper(data_for_path("."));
```

Obviously, this will be more interesting if your current directory contains subdirectories.

Displaying Recursively Defined Data

The Dumper routine of Data::Dumper displays the output nicely, but what if you don't like the format being used? You can write a routine to display the data. Again, for recursively defined data, a recursive subroutine is usually the key.

To dump the data, you need to know the name of the directory at the top of the tree because that's not stored within the structure:

```
sub dump_data_for_path {
  my $path = shift;
  my $data = shift;
  if (not defined $data) { # plain file
    print "$path\n";
    return;
  }
  ...
}
```

For a plain file, dump the pathname; for a directory, $data is a hash reference. Let's walk through the keys and dump the values:

```
sub dump_data_for_path {
  my $path = shift;
  my $data = shift;
  if (not defined $data) { # plain file
    print "$path\n";
    return;
  }
  my %directory = %$data;
  for (sort keys %directory) {
    dump_data_for_path("$path/$_", $directory{$_});
  }
}
```

For each element of the directory, you pass a path consisting of the incoming path followed by the current directory entry, and the data pointer is either undef for a file or a subdirectory hash reference for another directory. You can see the results by running:

```
dump_data_for_path(".", data_for_path("."));
```

Again, this is more interesting in a directory that has subdirectories, but the output should be similar to:

```
find . -print
```

from the shell prompt.

Exercises

The answers for all exercises can be found in the Appendix.

Exercise 1 [15 min]

Using the glob operator, a naïve sort of every name in the /bin directory by their relative sizes might be written as:

```
my @sorted = sort { -s $a <=> -s $b } glob "/bin/*";
```

Rewrite this using the Schwartzian Transform technique.

If you don't have many files in the /bin directory, perhaps because you don't have a Unix machine, change the argument to glob as needed.

Exercise 2 [15 min]

Read up on the Benchmark module, included with Perl. Write a program that will answer the question, "How much does using the Schwartzian Transform speed up the task of Exercise 1?"

Exercise 3 [10 min]

Using a Schwartzian Transform, read a list of words, and sort them in "dictionary order." Dictionary order ignores all capitalization and internal punctuation. Hint: The following transformation might be useful:

```
my $string = "Mary-Ann";
$string =~ tr/A-Z/a-z/;       # force all lowercase
$string =~ tr/a-z//cd;        # strip all but a-z from the string
print $string;                # prints "maryann"
```

Be sure you don't mangle the data! If the input includes the Professor, and The skipper, the output should have them listed in that order, with that capitalization.

Exercise 4 [20 min]

Modify the recursive directory dumping routine so it shows the nested directories through indentation. An empty directory should show up as:

```
sandbar, an empty directory
```

while a nonempty directory should appear with nested contents, indented two spaces:

```
uss_minnow, with contents:
  anchor
  broken_radio
  galley, with contents:
    captain_crunch_cereal
    gallon_of_milk
    tuna_fish_sandwich
  life_preservers
```

CHAPTER 8

Introduction to Objects

Object-oriented programming (often called OOP) helps programmers run code sooner and maintain it easier at the cost of making the resulting programs slower. That is to say, a typical program written in an OO language will normally run more slowly than the corresponding one written in a language without objects.

So why would anyone want their programs to run more slowly? Your programs will take less time to read, write, debug, and maintain, and on large projects, these factors are important. How much slowdown are we talking about? Well, that depends. But in general, the more heavily you use objects, the more it will save time for the programmer, and the more it will cost time at runtime. Still, you should remember that computers keep getting faster. Even if using OOP slows down your program, using next year's hardware will probably make up for it.

The benefits of OOP become worthwhile when your program (including all external libraries and modules) exceeds about N lines of code. Unfortunately, nobody can agree on what the value of N is, but for Perl programs, it's arguably around 1,000 lines of code. If your whole program is only be a couple hundred lines of code, using objects is probably a waste.

Like references, Perl's object architecture was grafted on after a substantial amount of existing pre-Perl5 code was already in use, so we had to ensure that it wouldn't break existing syntax. Amazingly, the only additional syntax to achieve object nirvana is the *method call*, introduced shortly. But the meaning of that syntax requires a bit of study, so let's proceed.

The Perl object architecture relies heavily on packages, subroutines, and references, so if you're skipping around in this book, please go back to the beginning. Ready? Here we go.

If We Could Talk to the Animals...

Obviously, the castaways can't survive on coconuts and pineapples alone. Luckily for them, a barge carrying random farm animals crashed on the island not long after they arrived, and the castaways began farming and raising animals.

Let's let those animals talk for a moment:

```perl
sub Cow::speak {
  print "a Cow goes moooo!\n";
}
sub Horse::speak {
  print "a Horse goes neigh!\n";
}
sub Sheep::speak {
  print "a Sheep goes baaaah!\n";
}

Cow::speak;
Horse::speak;
Sheep::speak;
```

This results in:

```
a Cow goes moooo!
a Horse goes neigh!
a Sheep goes baaaah!
```

Nothing spectacular here: simple subroutines, albeit from separate packages, and called using the full package name. Let's create an entire pasture:

```perl
sub Cow::speak {
  print "a Cow goes moooo!\n";
}
sub Horse::speak {
  print "a Horse goes neigh!\n";
}
sub Sheep::speak {
  print "a Sheep goes baaaah!\n";
}

my @pasture = qw(Cow Cow Horse Sheep Sheep);
foreach my $beast (@pasture) {
  &{$beast."::speak"};                    # Symbolic coderef
}
```

This results in:

```
a Cow goes moooo!
a Cow goes moooo!
a Horse goes neigh!
a Sheep goes baaaah!
a Sheep goes baaaah!
```

Wow. That symbolic coderef dereferencing there in the body of the loop is pretty nasty. We're counting on no strict 'refs' mode, certainly not recommended for larger programs.* And why was that necessary? Because the name of the package seems inseparable from the name of the subroutine you want to invoke within that package.

Or is it?

Introducing the Method Invocation Arrow

A *class* is a group of things with similar behaviors and traits. For now, let's say that Class->method invokes subroutine method in package Class. That's not completely accurate, but you'll catch on one step at a time. Let's use it like so:

```
sub Cow::speak {
  print "a Cow goes moooo!\n";
}
sub Horse::speak {
  print "a Horse goes neigh!\n";
}
sub Sheep::speak {
  print "a Sheep goes baaaah!\n";
}

Cow->speak;
Horse->speak;
Sheep->speak;
```

And once again, this results in:

```
a Cow goes moooo!
a Horse goes neigh!
a Sheep goes baaaah!
```

That's not fun yet. You've got the same number of characters, all constant, no variables. However, the parts are separable now:

```
my $beast = "Cow";
$beast->speak;              # invokes Cow->speak
```

Ahh! Now that the package name is separated from the subroutine name, you can use a variable package name. This time, you've got something that works even when use strict 'refs' is enabled.

Take the arrow invocation and put it back in the barnyard example:

```
sub Cow::speak {
  print "a Cow goes moooo!\n";
```

---

* Although all examples in this book should be valid Perl code, some examples in this chapter will break the rules enforced by use strict to make them easier to understand. By the end of the chapter, though, you'll learn how to make strict-compliant code again.

```
    }
    sub Horse::speak {
      print "a Horse goes neigh!\n";
    }
    sub Sheep::speak {
      print "a Sheep goes baaaah!\n";
    }

    my @pasture = qw(Cow Cow Horse Sheep Sheep);
    foreach my $beast (@pasture) {
      $beast->speak;
    }
```

There! Now all the animals are talking, and safely at that, without the use of symbolic coderefs.

But look at all that common code. Each speak routine has a similar structure: a print operator and a string that contains common text, except for two words. One of OOP's core features minimizes common code: if you write it only once, you'll save time. If you test and debug it only once, you'll save more time.

Now that you've learned more about what the method invocation arrow actually does, we've got an easier way to do the same thing.

The Extra Parameter of Method Invocation

The invocation of:

```
    Class->method(@args)
```

attempts to invoke the subroutine Class::method as:

```
    Class::method("Class", @args);
```

(If the subroutine can't be found, inheritance kicks in, but you'll learn about that later.) This means that you get the class name as the first parameter or the only parameter, if no arguments are given. You can rewrite the Sheep speaking subroutine as:

```
    sub Sheep::speak {
      my $class = shift;
      print "a $class goes baaaah!\n";
    }
```

The other two animals come out similarly:

```
    sub Cow::speak {
      my $class = shift;
      print "a $class goes moooo!\n";
    }
    sub Horse::speak {
      my $class = shift;
      print "a $class goes neigh!\n";
    }
```

In each case, $class gets the value appropriate for that subroutine. But once again, you have a lot of similar structure. Can you factor out that commonality even further? Yes—by calling another method in the same class.

Calling a Second Method to Simplify Things

You can call out from speak to a helper method called sound. This method provides the constant text for the sound itself:

```
{ package Cow;
  sub sound { "moooo" }
  sub speak {
    my $class = shift;
    print "a $class goes ", $class->sound, "!\n";
  }
}
```

Now, when you call Cow->speak, you get a $class of Cow in speak. This, in turn, selects the Cow->sound method, which returns moooo. How different would this be for the Horse?

```
{ package Horse;
  sub sound { "neigh" }
  sub speak {
    my $class = shift;
    print "a $class goes ", $class->sound, "!\n";
  }
}
```

Only the name of the package and the specific sound change. So can you share the definition for speak between the cow and the horse? Yes, with inheritance!

Now let's define a common subroutine package called Animal with the definition for speak:

```
{ package Animal;
  sub speak {
    my $class = shift;
    print "a $class goes ", $class->sound, "!\n";
  }
}
```

Then, for each animal, you can say it inherits from Animal, along with the animal-specific sound:

```
{ package Cow;
  @ISA = qw(Animal);
  sub sound { "moooo" }
}
```

Note the added @ISA array. We'll get to that in a minute.

What happens when you invoke Cow->speak now?

First, Perl constructs the argument list. In this case, it's just Cow. Then Perl looks for Cow::speak. That's not there, so Perl checks for the inheritance array @Cow::ISA. It's there, and contains the single name Animal.

Perl next checks for speak inside Animal instead, as in Animal::speak. That found, Perl invokes that subroutine with the already frozen argument list, as if you had said:

```
Animal::speak("Cow");
```

Inside the Animal::speak subroutine, $class becomes Cow as the first argument is shifted off. When you get to the step of invoking $class->sound while performing the print, it looks for Cow->sound:

```
print "a $class goes ", $class->sound, "!\n";
# but $class is Cow, so...
print "a Cow goes ", Cow->sound, "!\n";
# which invokes Cow->sound, returning "moooo", so
print "a Cow goes ", "moooo", "!\n";
```

and you get your desired output.

A Few Notes About @ISA

This magical @ISA variable (pronounced "is a" not "ice-uh"), declares that Cow "is a" Animal.* Note that it's an array, not a simple single value, because on rare occasions it makes sense to have more than one parent class searched for the missing methods. You'll learn more about that later.

If Animal also had an @ISA, you can check there too.† Typically, each @ISA has only one element (multiple elements means multiple inheritance and multiple head-aches), so you get a nice tree of inheritance. (There is also inheritance through UNIVERSAL and AUTOLOAD; see the perlobj manpage for the whole story.)

When you turn on use strict, you'll get complaints on @ISA because it's not a variable containing an explicit package name, nor is it a lexical (my) variable. You can't make it a lexical variable though: it has to belong to the package to be found by the inheritance mechanism.

There are a couple of straightforward ways to handle the declaration and setting of @ISA. The easiest is to just spell out the package name:

```
@Cow::ISA = qw(Animal);
```

You can also allow it as an implicitly named package variable:

```
package Cow;
use vars qw(@ISA);
@ISA = qw(Animal);
```

---

* ISA is actually a linguistic term. Once again, Larry Wall's background as a linguist has come back to influence Perl.

† The search is recursive, depth-first and left to right in each @ISA.

If you're on a recent-enough Perl (5.6 or later), you can use the our declaration to shorten it to:

```
package Cow;
our @ISA = qw(Animal);
```

However, if you think your code might be used by people stuck with Perl 5.005 or earlier, it's be best to avoid our.

If you're bringing in the class from outside, via an object-oriented module, change:

```
package Cow;
use Animal;
use vars qw(@ISA);
@ISA = qw(Animal);
```

to just:

```
package Cow;
use base qw(Animal);
```

That's pretty darn compact. Furthermore, use base has the advantage that it's performed at compile time, eliminating a few potential errors from setting @ISA at runtime, like some of the other solutions.

Overriding the Methods

Let's add a mouse that can barely be heard:

```
{ package Animal;
  sub speak {
    my $class = shift;
    print "a $class goes ", $class->sound, "!\n";
  }
}
{ package Mouse;
  @ISA = qw(Animal);
  sub sound { "squeak" }
  sub speak {
    my $class = shift;
    print "a $class goes ", $class->sound, "!\n";
    print "[but you can barely hear it!]\n";
  }
}

Mouse->speak;
```

which results in:

```
a Mouse goes squeak!
[but you can barely hear it!]
```

Here, Mouse has its own speaking routine, so Mouse->speak doesn't immediately invoke Animal->speak. This is known as *overriding*. You use overriding to shadow the method in the derived class (Mouse) because you have a specialized version of the routine, instead of calling the more general base class's method (in `Animal`). In fact, you didn't even need to initialize `@Mouse::ISA` to say that a `Mouse` was an `Animal` at all because all the methods needed for speak are defined completely with `Mouse`.

You've now duplicated some of the code from `Animal->speak`; this can be a maintenance headache. For example, suppose someone decides that the word goes in the output of the `Animal` class is a bug. Now the maintainer of that class changes goes to says. Your mice will still say goes, which means the code still has the bug. The problem is that you invoked cut and paste to duplicate code, and in OOP, that is a sin. You should reuse code through inheritance, not by cut and paste.

How can you avoid that? Can you say somehow that a `Mouse` does everything any other `Animal` does, but add in the extra comment? Sure!

As your first attempt, you can invoke the `Animal::speak` method directly:

```
{ package Animal;
  sub speak {
    my $class = shift;
    print "a $class goes ", $class->sound, "!\n";
  }
}
{ package Mouse;
  @ISA = qw(Animal);
  sub sound { "squeak" }
  sub speak {
    my $class = shift;
    Animal::speak($class);
    print "[but you can barely hear it!]\n";
  }
}
```

Note that because you've stopped using the method arrow, you have to include the `$class` parameter (almost surely the value of `"Mouse"`) as the first parameter to `Animal::speak`,.

Why did you stop using the arrow? Well, if you invoke `Animal->speak` there, the first parameter to the method is `"Animal,"` not `"Mouse"`, and when the time comes for it to call for the sound, it won't have the right class to select the proper methods for this object.

Invoking `Animal::speak` directly is a mess, however. What if `Animal::speak` didn't exist before and was inherited from a class mentioned in `@Animal::ISA`? For example, suppose the code was:

```
{ package LivingCreature;
  sub speak { ... }
  ...
}
{ package Animal;
  @ISA = qw(LivingCreature);
  # no definition for speak( )
```

```
      ...
  }
  { package Mouse;
    @ISA = qw(Animal);
    sub speak {
      ...
      Animal::speak(  ... );
    }
    ...
  }
```

Because you no longer use the method arrow, you get one and only one chance to hit the right subroutine. You'll look for it in `Animal`, and not find it, and the program aborts.

The `Animal` classname is now hardwired into the subroutine selection. This is a mess if someone maintains the code, changing `@ISA` for `Mouse`, and didn't notice `Animal` there in speak. Thus, this is probably not the right way to go.

Starting the Search from a Different Place

A better solution is to tell Perl to search from a different place in the inheritance chain:

```
  { package Animal;
    sub speak {
      my $class = shift;
      print "a $class goes ", $class->sound, "!\n";
    }
  }
  { package Mouse;
    @ISA = qw(Animal);
    sub sound { "squeak" }
    sub speak {
      my $class = shift;
      $class->Animal::speak(@_);
      print "[but you can barely hear it!]\n";
    }
  }
```

Ahh. As ugly as this is, it works. Using this syntax, start with `Animal` to find speak and use all of `Animal`'s inheritance chain if not found immediately. The first parameter is `$class` (because you're using an arrow again), so the found speak method gets `Mouse` as its first entry and eventually works its way back to `Mouse::sound` for the details.

This isn't the best solution, however. You still have to keep the `@ISA` and the initial search package in sync (changes in one must be considered for changes in the other). Worse, if `Mouse` had multiple entries in `@ISA`, you wouldn't necessarily know which one had actually defined speak.

So, is there an even better way?

The SUPER Way of Doing Things

By changing the `Animal` class to the `SUPER` class in that invocation, you get a search of all your superclasses (classes listed in `@ISA`) automatically:

```perl
{ package Animal;
  sub speak {
    my $class = shift;
    print "a $class goes ", $class->sound, "!\n";
  }
}
{ package Mouse;
  @ISA = qw(Animal);
  sub sound { "squeak" }
  sub speak {
    my $class = shift;
    $class->SUPER::speak;
    print "[but you can barely hear it!]\n";
  }
}
```

Thus, `SUPER::speak` means to look in the current package's `@ISA` for speak, invoking the first one found if there's more than one. In this case, you look in the one and only base class, `Animal`, find `Animal::speak`, and pass it `"Mouse"` as its only parameter.

What to Do with @_

In that last example, had there been any additional parameters to the speak routine (like how many times, or in what pitch for singing, for example), the parameters would be ignored by the `Mouse::speak` routine. If you want them to be passed uninterpreted to the parent class, you can add it as a parameter:

```perl
$class->SUPER::speak(@_);
```

This invokes the speak routine of the parent class, including all the parameters that you've not yet shifted off of your parameter list.

Which one is correct? It depends. If you are writing a class that simply adds to some of the parent class behavior, it's best to simply pass along arguments you haven't dealt with. However, if you want precise control over the parent class behavior, you should determine the argument list explicitly, and pass it.

Where We Are So Far...

So far, you've seen the method arrow syntax:

```perl
Class->method(@args);
```

or the equivalent:

```
my $beast = "Class";
$beast->method(@args);
```

which constructs an argument list of:

```
("Class", @args)
```

and attempts to invoke:

```
Class::method("Class", @args);
```

However, if `Class::method` is not found, `@Class::ISA` is examined (recursively) to locate a package that does indeed contain `method`, and that subroutine is invoked instead.

Chapter 9 shows how to distinguish the individual animals by giving them associated properties, called *instance variables*.

Exercises

The answers for all exercises can be found in the Appendix.

Exercise 1 [20 min]

Type in the `Animal`, `Cow`, `Horse`, `Sheep`, and `Mouse` class definitions. Make it work with use strict. Use our if you're using a recent enough version of Perl. Your program should ask the user to enter the names of one or more barnyard animals. Create a barnyard with those animals, and have each animal speak once.

Exercise 2 [40 min]

Add a `Person` class at the same level as `Animal`, and have both of them inherit from a new class called `LivingCreature`. Also make the speak method take a parameter of what to say, falling back to the sound (humming for a `Person`) if no parameter is given. Since this isn't Dr. Doolittle, make sure the animals can't talk. (That is, don't let speak have any parameters for an animal.) Try not to duplicate any code, but be sure to catch likely errors of usage, such as forgetting to define a sound for an animal.

Demonstrate the `Person` class by invoking a person with nothing to say, and then demonstrate it a second time by invoking a person with something to say.

Objects with Data

Using the simple syntax introduced in Chapter 8, you have class methods, (multiple) inheritance, overriding, and extending. You've been able to factor out common code and provide a way to reuse implementations with variations. This is at the core of what objects provide, but objects also provide *instance data*, which we haven't even begun to cover.

A Horse Is a Horse, of Course of Course—or Is It?

Let's look at the code used in Chapter 8 for the Animal classes and Horse classes:

```
{ package Animal;
  sub speak {
    my $class = shift;
    print "a $class goes ", $class->sound, "!\n"
  }
}
{ package Horse;
  @ISA = qw(Animal);
  sub sound { "neigh" }
}
```

This lets you invoke Horse->speak to ripple upward to Animal::speak, calling back to Horse::sound to get the specific sound, and the output of:

```
a Horse goes neigh!
```

But all Horse objects would have to be absolutely identical. If you add a subroutine, all horses automatically share it. That's great for making horses identical, but how do you capture the properties of an individual horse? For example, suppose you want to give your horse a name. There's got to be a way to keep its name separate from those of other horses.

You can do so by establishing an instance. An *instance* is generally created by a class, much like a car is created by a car factory. An instance will have associated properties, called *instance variables* (or member variables, if you come from a C++ or Java background). An instance has a unique identity (like the serial number of a registered horse), shared properties (the color and talents of the horse), and common behavior (i.e., pulling the reins back tells the horse to stop).

In Perl, an instance must be a reference to one of the built-in types. Start with the simplest reference that can hold a horse's name: a scalar reference:[*]

```
my $name = "Mr. Ed";
my $tv_horse = \$name;
```

Now $tv_horse is a reference to what will be the instance-specific data (the name). The final step in turning this into a real instance involves a special operator called bless:

```
bless $tv_horse, "Horse";
```

The bless operator follows the reference to find what variable it points to—in this case the scalar $name. Then it "blesses" that variable, turning $tv_horse into an object —a Horse object, in fact. (Imagine that a little sticky-note that says Horse is now attached to $name.)

At this point, $tv_horse is an instance of Horse.[†] That is, it's a specific horse. The reference is otherwise unchanged and can still be used with traditional dereferencing operators.[‡]

Invoking an Instance Method

The method arrow can be used on instances, as well as names of packages (classes). Let's get the sound that $tv_horse makes:

```
my $noise = $tv_horse->sound;
```

To invoke sound, Perl first notes that $tv_horse is a blessed reference, and thus an instance. Perl then constructs an argument list, similar to the way an argument list was constructed when you used the method arrow with a class name. In this case, it'll be just ($tv_horse). (Later you'll see that arguments will take their place following the instance variable, just as with classes.)

Now for the fun part: Perl takes the class in which the instance was blessed, in this case Horse, and uses it to locate the subroutine to invoke the method, as if you had

---

[*] The simplest, but rarely used in real code for reasons you'll see shortly

[†] Actually, $tv_horse points to the object, but in common terms, you nearly always deal with objects by references to those objects. Hence, it's simpler to say that $tv_horse is the horse, not "the thing that $tv_horse is referencing."

[‡] Although doing so outside the class is a bad idea, as you'll see later.

said Horse->sound instead of $tv_horse->sound. The purpose of the original blessing is to associate a class with that reference to allow the proper method (subroutine) to be found.

In this case, Horse::sound is found directly (without using inheritance), yielding the final subroutine invocation:

```
Horse::sound($tv_horse)
```

Note that the first parameter here is still the instance, not the name of the class as before. neigh is the return value, which ends up as the earlier $noise variable.

If Horse::sound had not been found, you'd wander up the @Horse::ISA list to try to find the method in one of the superclasses, just as for a class method. The only difference between a class method and an instance method is whether the first parameter is an instance (a blessed reference) or a class name (a string).*

Accessing the Instance Data

Because you get the instance as the first parameter, you can now access the instance-specific data. In this case, let's add a way to get at the name:

```
{ package Horse;
  @ISA = qw(Animal);
  sub sound { "neigh" }
  sub name {
    my $self = shift;
    $$self;
  }
}
```

Now you call for the name:

```
print $tv_horse->name, " says ", $tv_horse->sound, "\n";
```

Inside Horse::name, the @_ array contains just $tv_horse, which the shift stores into $self. It's traditional to shift the first parameter into a variable named $self for instance methods, so stay with that unless you have strong reasons otherwise. Perl places no significance on the name $self, however.†

Then $self is dereferenced as a scalar reference, yielding Mr. Ed. The result is:

```
Mr. Ed says neigh.
```

---

* This is perhaps different from other OOP languages with which you may be familiar.

† If you come from another OO language background, you might choose $this or $me for the variable name, but you'll probably confuse most other Perl OO-hackers.

How to Build a Horse

If you constructed all your horses by hand, you'd most likely make mistakes from time to time. Making the "inside guts" of a Horse visible also violates one of the principles of OOP. That's good if you're a veterinarian but not if you just like to own horses. Let the Horse class build a new horse:

```
{ package Horse;
  @ISA = qw(Animal);
  sub sound { "neigh" }
  sub name {
    my $self = shift;
    $$self;
  }
  sub named {
    my $class = shift;
    my $name = shift;
    bless \$name, $class;
  }
}
```

Now with the new named method, build a Horse:

```
my $tv_horse = Horse->named("Mr. Ed");
```

You're back to a class method, so the two arguments to Horse::named are "Horse" and "Mr. Ed". The bless operator not only blesses $name, it also returns the reference to $name, so that's fine as a return value. And that's how to build a horse.

You called the constructor named here so it quickly denotes the constructor's argument as the name for this particular Horse. You can use different constructors with different names for different ways of "giving birth" to the object (such as recording its pedigree or date of birth). However, you'll find that most people coming to Perl from less-flexible languages (such as Java or C++) use a single constructor named new, with various ways of interpreting the arguments to new. Either style is fine, as long as you document your particular way of giving birth to an object. Most core and CPAN modules use new, with notable exceptions, such as DBI's DBI->connect( ). It's really up to the author. It all works, as long as it's documented.

Inheriting the Constructor

Was there anything specific to Horse in that method? No. Therefore, it's also the same recipe for building anything else inherited from Animal, so let's put it there:

```
{ package Animal;
  sub speak {
    my $class = shift;
    print "a $class goes ", $class->sound, "!\n"
  }
  sub name {
```

```
      my $self = shift;
      $$self;
    }
    sub named {
      my $class = shift;
      my $name = shift;
      bless \$name, $class;
    }
  }
  { package Horse;
    @ISA = qw(Animal);
    sub sound { "neigh" }
  }
```

Ahh, but what happens if you invoke speak on an instance?

```
my $tv_horse = Horse->named("Mr. Ed");
$tv_horse->speak;
```

You get a debugging value:

```
a Horse=SCALAR(0xaca42ac) goes neigh!
```

Why? Because the Animal::speak routine expects a classname as its first parameter,
not an instance. When the instance is passed in, you'll use a blessed scalar reference
as a string, which shows up as you saw it just now—similar to a stringified reference, but with the class name in front.

Making a Method Work with Either Classes
or Instances

All you need to fix this is a way to detect whether the method is called on a class or
an instance. The most straightforward way to find out is with the ref operator. This
operator returns a string (the classname) when used on a blessed reference, and undef
when used on a string (like a classname). Modify the name method first to notice the
change:

```
sub name {
  my $either = shift;
  ref $either
    ? $$either              # it's an instance, return name
    : "an unnamed $either"; # it's a class, return generic
}
```

Here the ?: operator selects either the dereference or a derived string. Now you can
use it with either an instance or a class. Note that you changed the first parameter
holder to $either to show that it is intentional:

```
print Horse->name, "\n";      # prints "an unnamed Horse\n"

my $tv_horse = Horse->named("Mr. Ed");
print $tv_horse->name, "\n";   # prints "Mr Ed.\n"
```

and now you'll fix speak to use this:

```perl
sub speak {
  my $either = shift;
  print $either->name, " goes ", $either->sound, "\n";
}
```

Since sound already worked with either a class or an instance, you're done!

Adding Parameters to a Method

Let's train your animals to eat:

```perl
{ package Animal;
  sub named {
    my $class = shift;
    my $name = shift;
    bless \$name, $class;
  }
  sub name {
    my $either = shift;
    ref $either
      ? $$either # it's an instance, return name
      : "an unnamed $either"; # it's a class, return generic
  }
  sub speak {
    my $either = shift;
    print $either->name, " goes ", $either->sound, "\n";
  }
  sub eat {
    my $either = shift;
    my $food = shift;
    print $either->name, " eats $food.\n";
  }
}
{ package Horse;
  @ISA = qw(Animal);
  sub sound { "neigh" }
}
{ package Sheep;
  @ISA = qw(Animal);
  sub sound { "baaaah" }
}
```

Now try it out:

```perl
my $tv_horse = Horse->named("Mr. Ed");
$tv_horse->eat("hay");
Sheep->eat("grass");
```

It prints:

```
Mr. Ed eats hay.
an unnamed Sheep eats grass.
```

An instance method with parameters gets invoked with the instance, and then the list of parameters. That first invocation is like:

```
Animal::eat($tv_horse, "hay");
```

The instance methods form the *Application Programming Interface* (API) for an object. Most of the effort involved in designing a good object class goes into the API design because the API defines how reusable and maintainable the object and its subclasses will be. Do not rush to freeze an API design before you've considered how the object will be used.

More Interesting Instances

What if an instance needs more data? Most interesting instances are made of many items, each of which can in turn be a reference or another object. The easiest way to store these items is often in a hash. The keys of the hash serve as the names of parts of the object (also called instance or member variables), and the corresponding values are, well, the values.

How do you turn the horse into a hash?* Recall that an object is any blessed reference. You can just as easily make it a blessed hash reference as a blessed scalar reference, as long as everything that looks at the reference is changed accordingly.

Let's make a sheep that has a name and a color:

```
my $lost = bless { Name => "Bo", Color => "white" }, Sheep;
```

$lost->{Name} has Bo, and $lost->{Color} has white. But you want to make $lost->name access the name, and that's now messed up because it's expecting a scalar reference. Not to worry, because it's pretty easy to fix up:

```
## in Animal
sub name {
  my $either = shift;
  ref $either
    ? $either->{Name}
    : "an unnamed $either";
}
```

named still builds a scalar sheep, so let's fix that as well:

```
## in Animal
sub named {
  my $class = shift;
  my $name = shift;
  my $self = { Name => $name, Color => $class->default_color };
  bless $self, $class;
}
```

---

* Other than calling on a butcher, that is.

What's this `default_color`? If `named` has only the name, you still need to set a color, so you'll have a class-specific initial color. For a sheep, you might define it as white:

```
## in Sheep
sub default_color { "white" }
```

Then to keep from having to define one for each additional class, define a backstop method, which serves as the "default default," directly in `Animal`:

```
## in Animal
sub default_color { "brown" }
```

Thus, all animals are brown (muddy, perhaps), unless a specific animal class gives a specific override to this method.

Now, because `name` and `named` were the only methods that referenced the structure of the object, the remaining methods can stay the same, so `speak` still works as before. This supports another basic rule of OOP: if the structure of the object is accessed only by the object's own methods or inherited methods, there's less code to change when it's time to modify that structure.

A Horse of a Different Color

Having all horses be brown would be boring. Let's add a method or two to get and set the color:

```
## in Animal
sub color {
  my $self = shift;
  $self->{Color};
}
sub set_color {
  my $self = shift;
  $self->{Color} = shift;
}
```

Now you can fix that color for Mr. Ed:

```
my $tv_horse = Horse->named("Mr. Ed");
$tv_horse->set_color("black-and-white");
print $tv_horse->name, " is colored ", $tv_horse->color, "\n";
```

which results in:

```
Mr. Ed is colored black-and-white
```

Getting Your Deposit Back

Because of the way the code is written, the setter also returns the updated value. Think about this (and document it) when you write a setter. What does the setter return? Here are some common variations:

- The updated parameter (same as what was passed in)
- The previous value (similar to the way umask or the single-argument form of select works)
- The object itself
- A success/fail code

Each has advantages and disadvantages. For example, if you return the updated parameter, you can use it again for another object:

```
$tv_horse->set_color( $eating->set_color( color_from_user() ));
```

The implementation given earlier returns the newly updated value. Frequently, this is the easiest code to write, and often the fastest to execute.

If you return the previous parameter, you can easily create "set this value temporarily to that" functions:

```
{
  my $old_color = $tv_horse->set_color("orange");
  ... do things with $tv_horse ...
  $tv_horse->set_color($old_color);
}
```

This is implemented as:

```
sub set_color {
  my $self = shift;
  my $old = $self->{Color};
  $self->{Color} = shift;
  $old;
}
```

For more efficiency, you can avoid stashing the previous value when in a void context using the wantarray function:

```
sub set_color {
  my $self = shift;
  if (defined wantarray) {
    # this method call is not in void context, so
    # the return value matters
    my $old = $self->{Color};
    $self->{Color} = shift;
    $old;
  } else {
    # this method call is in void context
    $self->{Color} = shift;
  }
}
```

If you return the object itself, you can chain settings:

```
my $tv_horse =
  Horse->named("Mr. Ed")
       ->set_color("grey")
       ->set_age(4)
       ->set_height("17 hands");
```

This works because the output of each setter is the original object, becoming the object for the next method call. Implementing this is again relatively easy:

```
sub set_color {
  my $self = shift;
  $self->{Color} = shift;
  $self;
}
```

The void context trick can be used here too, although with questionable value because you've already established $self.

Finally, returning a success status is useful if it's fairly common for an update to fail, rather than an exceptional event. The other variations would have to indicate failure by throwing an exception with die.

In summary: use what you want, be consistent if you can, but document it nonetheless (and don't change it after you've already released one version).

Don't Look Inside the Box

You might have obtained or set the color outside the class simply by following the hash reference: $tv_horse->{Color}. However, this violates the *encapsulation* of the object by exposing its internal structure. The object is supposed to be a black box, but you've pried off the hinges and looked inside.

One purpose of OOP is to enable the maintainer of Animal or Horse to make reasonably independent changes to the implementation of the methods and still have the exported interface work properly. To see why accessing the hash directly violates this, let's say that Animal no longer uses a simple color name for the color, but instead changes to use a computed RGB triple to store the color (holding it as an arrayref), as in:

```
use Color::Conversions qw(color_name_to_rgb rgb_to_color_name);
...
sub set_color {
  my $self = shift;
  my $new_color = shift;
  $self->{Color} = color_name_to_rgb($new_color);  # arrayref
}
sub color {
  my $self = shift;
  rgb_to_color_name($self->{Color});                # takes arrayref
}
```

The old interface can be maintained if you use a setter and getter because they can perform the translations. You can also add new interfaces now to enable the direct setting and getting of the RGB triple:

```
sub set_color_rgb {
  my $self = shift;
```

```
    $self->{Color} = [@_];                  # set colors to remaining parameters
  }
  sub get_color_rgb {
    my $self = shift;
    @{ $self->{Color} };                     # return RGB list
  }
```

If you use code outside the class that looks at $tv_horse->{Color} directly, this change is no longer possible. Store a string ('blue') where an arrayref is needed ([0,0,255]) or use an arrayref as a string.

Faster Getters and Setters

Because you're going to play nice and always call the getters and setters instead of reaching into the data structure, getters and setters are called frequently. To save a teeny-tiny bit of time, you might see these getters and setters written as:

```
## in Animal
sub color {
  $_[0]->{Color}
}
sub set_color {
  $_[0]->{Color} = $_[1];
}
```

Here's an alternate way to access the arguments: $_[0] is used in place, rather than with a shift. Functionally, this example is identical to the previous implementation, but it's slightly faster, at the expense of some ugliness.

Getters That Double as Setters

Another alternative to the pattern of creating two different methods for getting and setting a parameter is to create one method that notes whether or not it gets any additional arguments. If the arguments are absent, it's a get operation; if the arguments are present, it's a set operation. A simple version looks like:

```
sub color {
  my $shift;
  if (@_) {                    # are there any more parameters?
    # yes, it's a setter:
    $self->{Color} = shift;
  } else {
    # no, it's a getter:
    $self->{Color};
  }
}
```

Now you can say:

```
my $tv_horse = Horse->named("Mr. Ed");
$tv_horse->color("black-and-white");
print $tv_horse->name, " is colored ", $tv_horse->color, "\n";
```

The presence of the parameter in the second line denotes that you are setting the color, while its absence in the third line indicates a getter.

While this strategy might at first seem attractive because of its apparent simplicity, it complicates the actions of the getter (which will be called frequently). This strategy also makes it difficult to search through your listings to find only the setters of a particular parameter, which are often more important than the getters. In fact, we've been burned by this in the past when a setter became a getter because another function returned more parameters than expected after an upgrade.

Restricting a Method to Class-Only or Instance-Only

Setting the name of an unnameable generic Horse is probably not a good idea; neither is calling named on an instance. Nothing in the Perl subroutine definition says "this is a class method" or "this is an instance method." Fortunately, the ref operator lets you throw an exception when called incorrectly. As an example of instance- or class-only methods, consider the following:

```
use Carp qw(croak);

sub instance_only {
  ref(my $self = shift) or croak "instance variable needed";
  ... use $self as the instance ...
}

sub class_only {
  ref(my $class = shift) and croak "class name needed";
  ... use $class as the class ...
}
```

Here, the ref function returns true for an instance or false for a class. If the undesired value is returned, you'll croak, which has the added advantage of placing the blame on the caller, not on you. The caller will get an error message like this, giving the line number in their code where the wrong method was called:

```
instance variable needed at their_code line 1234
```

While this seems like a good thing to do all the time, practically no CPAN or core modules add this extra checking. Maybe it's only for the ultra-paranoid.

Exercise

The answers for all exercises can be found in the Appendix.

Exercise [45 min]

Give the Animal class the ability to get and set the name and color. Be sure that your result works under use strict. Also make sure your get methods work with both a generic animal and a specific animal instance. Test your work with:

```
my $tv_horse = Horse->named("Mr. Ed");
$tv_horse->set_name("Mister Ed");
$tv_horse->set_color("grey");
print $tv_horse->name, " is ", $tv_horse->color, "\n";
print Sheep->name, " colored ", Sheep->color, " goes ", Sheep->sound, "\n";
```

What should you do if you're asked to set the name or color of a generic animal?

CHAPTER 10

Object Destruction

In the previous two chapters, we looked at basic object creation and manipulation. In this chapter, we'll look at an equally important topic: what happens when objects go away.

As you saw in Chapter 4, when the last reference to a Perl data structure goes away, Perl automatically reclaims the memory of that data structure, including destroying any links to other data. Of course, that in turn may cause other ("contained") structures to be destroyed as well.

By default, objects work in this manner because objects use the same reference structure to make more complex objects. An object built of a hash reference is destroyed when the last reference to that hash goes away. If the values of the hash elements are also references, they're similarly removed, possibly causing further destruction.

Suppose an object uses a temporary file to hold data that won't fit entirely in memory. The filehandle for this temporary file can be included as one of the object's instance variables. While the normal object destruction sequence will properly close the handle, you still have the temporary file on disk unless you take further action.

To perform the proper cleanup operations when an object is destroyed, you need to be notified when that happens. Thankfully, Perl provides such notification upon request. You can request this notification by giving the object a DESTROY method.

When the last reference to an object, say $bessie, is destroyed, Perl invokes:

```
$bessie->DESTROY
```

This method call is like most other method calls: Perl starts at the class of the object and works its way up the inheritance hierarchy until it finds a suitable method. However, unlike other method calls, there's no error if no suitable method is found.*

---

* Normally, your own method calls will cause an error if the method isn't found. If you want to prevent that, just put a do-nothing method into the base class.

For example, going back to the Animal class defined in Chapter 9, you can add a DESTROY method to know when objects go away, purely for debugging purposes:

```
## in Animal
sub DESTROY {
  my $self = shift;
  print "[", $self->name, " has died.]\n";
}
```

Now when you create any Animals in the program, you get notification as they leave. For example:

```
## include animal classes from previous chapter...

sub feed_a_cow_named {
  my $name = shift;
  my $cow = Cow->named($name);
  $cow->eat("grass");
  print "Returning from the subroutine.\n";    # $cow is destroyed here
}
print "Start of program.\n";
my $outer_cow = Cow->named("Bessie");
print "Now have a cow named ", $outer_cow->name, ".\n";
feed_a_cow_named("Gwen");
print "Returned from subroutine.\n";
```

This prints:

```
Start of program.
Now have a cow named Bessie.
Gwen eats grass.
Returning from the subroutine.
[Gwen has died.]
Returned from subroutine.
[Bessie has died.]
```

Note that Gwen is active inside the subroutine. However, as the subroutine exits, Perl notices there are no references to Gwen; Gwen's DESTROY method is then automatically invoked, printing the Gwen has died message.

What happens at the end of the program? Since objects don't live beyond the end of the program, Perl makes one final pass over all remaining data and destroys it. This is true whether the data is held in lexical variables or package global variables. Because Bessie was still alive at the end of the program, she needed to be recycled, and so you get the message for Bessie after all other steps in the program are complete.[*]

---

[*] This is just after the END blocks are executed and follows the same rules as END blocks: there must be a nice exit of the program rather than an abrupt end. If Perl runs out of memory, all bets are off.

Nested Object Destruction

If an object holds another object (say, as an element of an array or the value of a hash element), the containing object is DESTROYed before any of the contained objects begin their discarding process. This is reasonable because the containing object may need to reference its contents in order to be cleanly discarded. To illustrate this, let's build a "barn" and tear it down. And just to be interesting, we'll make the barn a blessed array reference, not a hash reference.

```
{ package Barn;
  sub new { bless [ ], shift }
  sub add { push @{+shift}, shift }
  sub contents { @{+shift} }
  sub DESTROY {
    my $self = shift;
    print "$self is being destroyed...\n";
    for ($self->contents) {
      print "  ", $_->name, " goes homeless.\n";
    }
  }
}
```

Here, we're really being minimalistic in the object definition. To create a new barn, simply bless an empty array reference into the class name passed as the first parameter. Adding an animal just pushes it to the back of the barn. Asking for the barn contents merely dereferences the object array reference to return the contents.*

The fun part is the destructor. Let's take the reference to ourselves, display a debugging message about the particular barn being destroyed, and then ask for the name of each inhabitant in turn. In action, this would be:

```
my $barn = Barn->new;
$barn->add(Cow->named("Bessie"));
$barn->add(Cow->named("Gwen"));
print "Burn the barn:\n";
$barn = undef;
print "End of program.\n";
```

This prints:

```
Burn the barn:
Barn=ARRAY(0x541c) is being destroyed...
  Bessie goes homeless.
  Gwen goes homeless.
[Gwen has died.]
[Bessie has died.]
End of program.
```

---

* Did you wonder why there's a plus sign (+) before shift in two of those subroutines? That's due to one of the quirks in Perl's syntax. If the code were simply @{shift}, because the curly braces contain nothing but a bareword, it would be interpreted as a soft reference: @{"shift"}. In Perl, the unary plus (a plus sign at the beginning of a term) is defined to do nothing (not even turning what follows into a number), just so it can distinguish cases such as this.

Note that the barn is destroyed first, letting you get the name of the inhabitants cleanly. However, once the barn is gone, the inhabitants have no additional references, so they also go away, and thus their destructors are also invoked. Compare that with the cows having a life outside the barn:

```
my $barn = Barn->new;
my @cows = (Cow->named("Bessie"), Cow->named("Gwen"));
$barn->add($_) for @cows;
print "Burn the barn:\n";
$barn = undef;
print "Lose the cows:\n";
@cows = ( );
print "End of program.\n";
```

This produces:

```
Burn the barn:
Barn=ARRAY(0x541c) is being destroyed...
  Bessie goes homeless.
  Gwen goes homeless.
Lose the cows:
[Gwen has died.]
[Bessie has died.]
End of program.
```

The cows will now continue to live until the only other reference to the cows (from the @cows array) goes away.

The references to the cows are removed only when the barn destructor is completely finished. In some cases, you may wish instead to shoo the cows out of the barn as you notice them. In this case, it's as simple as destructively altering the barn array, rather than iterating over it.* Let's alter the Barn to Barn2 to illustrate this:

```
{ package Barn2;
  sub new { bless [ ], shift }
  sub add { push @{+shift}, shift }
  sub contents { @{+shift} }
  sub DESTROY {
    my $self = shift;
    print "$self is being destroyed...\n";
    while (@$self) {
      my $homeless = shift @$self;
      print "  ", $homeless->name, " goes homeless.\n";
    }
  }
}
```

Now use it in the previous scenarios:

```
my $barn = Barn2->new;
$barn->add(Cow->named("Bessie"));
```

---

* If you're using a hash instead, use delete on the elements you wish to process immediately.

```
$barn->add(Cow->named("Gwen"));
print "Burn the barn:\n";
$barn = undef;
print "End of program.\n";
```

This produces:

```
Burn the barn:
Barn2=ARRAY(0x541c) is being destroyed...
  Bessie goes homeless.
[Bessie has died.]
  Gwen goes homeless.
[Gwen has died.]
End of program.
```

As you can see, Bessie had no home by being booted out of the barn immediately, so she also died. (Poor Gwen suffers the same fate.) There were no references to her at that moment, even before the destructor for the barn was complete.

Thus, back to the temporary file problem. If you have an associated temporary file for an animal, you merely need to close it and delete the file during the destructor:

```
## in Animal
use File::Temp qw(tempfile);

sub named {
  my $class = shift;
  my $name = shift;
  my $self = { Name => $name, Color => $class->default_color };
  ## new code here...
  my ($fh, $filename) = tempfile();
  $self->{temp_fh} = $fh;
  $self->{temp_filename} = $filename;
  ## .. to here
  bless $self, $class;
}
```

You now have a filehandle and its filename stored as instance variables of the Animal (or any class derived from Animal). In the destructor, close it down, and delete the file:*

```
sub DESTROY {
  my $self = shift;
  my $fh = $self->{temp_fh};
  close $fh;
  unlink $self->{temp_filename};
  print "[", $self->name, " has died.]\n";
}
```

---

* As it turns out, you can tell File::Temp to do this automatically, but then we wouldn't be able to illustrate doing it manually. Doing it manually allows you to store a summary of the information from the temporary file into a database. However, that's too complex to show here.

When the last reference to the Animal-ish object is destroyed (even at the end of the program), also automatically remove the temporary file to avoid a mess.

Beating a Dead Horse

Because the destructor method is inherited, you can also override and extend superclass methods. For example, we'll decide the dead horses need a further use:

```
## in Horse
sub DESTROY {
  my $self = shift;
  $self->SUPER::DESTROY;
  print "[", $self->name, " has gone off to the glue factory.]\n";
}

my @tv_horses = map Horse->named($_), ("Trigger", "Mr. Ed");
$_->eat("an apple") for @tv_horses;      # their last meal
print "End of program.\n";
```

This prints:

```
Trigger eats an apple.
Mr. Ed eats an apple.
End of program.
[Mr. Ed has died.]
[Mr. Ed has gone off to the glue factory.]
[Trigger has died.]
[Trigger has gone off to the glue factory.]
```

We'll feed each horse a last meal; at the end of the program, each horse's destructor is called.

The first step of this destructor is to call the parent destructor. Why is this important? Without calling the parent destructor, the steps taken by superclasses of this class will not properly execute. That's not much if it's simply a debugging statement as we've shown, but if it was the "delete the temporary file" cleanup method, you wouldn't have deleted that file!

So, the rule is:

> *Always include a call to* $self->SUPER::DESTROY *in your destructors (even if you don't yet have any base/parent classes).*

Whether you call it at the beginning or the end of your own destructor is a matter of hotly contested debate. If your derived class needs some superclass instance variables, you should probably call the superclass destructor after you complete your operations because the superclass destructor will likely alter them in annoying ways. On the other hand, in the example, we called the superclass destructor before the added behavior, because we wanted the superclass behavior first. There's no rule of thumb, even. Sorry.

Indirect Object Notation

The arrow syntax used to invoke a method is sometimes called the *direct object* syntax because there's also the *indirect object* syntax, also known as the "only works sometimes" syntax, for reasons explained in a moment. When you write:

```
Class->class_method(@args);
$instance->instance_method(@other);
```

you can generally replace it with:

```
classmethod Class @args;
instancemethod $instance @other;
```

A typical use of this is with the new method, replacing:

```
my $obj = Some::Class->new(@constructor_params);
```

with:

```
my $obj = new Some::Class @constructor_params;
```

making the C++ people feel right at home. Of course, in Perl, there's nothing special about the name new, but at least the syntax is hauntingly familiar.

Why the previous "generally" caveat? Well, if the instance is something more complicated than a simple scalar variable:

```
$somehash->{$somekey}->[42]->instance_method(@parms);
```

then you can't just swap it around like:

```
instance_method $somehash->{$somekey}->[42] @parms;
```

because the only things acceptable to indirect object syntax are a bareword (e.g., a class name), a simple scalar variable, or braces denoting a block returning either a blessed reference or a classname.* This means you have to write it like so:

```
instance_method { $somehash->{$somekey}->[42] } @parms;
```

And that goes from simple to uglier in one step. There's another downside: ambiguous parsing. When we developed the classroom materials concerning indirect object references, we wrote:

```
my $cow = Cow->named("Bessie");
print name $cow, " eats.\n";
```

because we were thinking about the indirect object equivalents for:

```
my $cow = Cow->named("Bessie");
print $cow->name, " eats.\n";
```

---

* Astute readers will note that these are the same rules as for an indirect filehandle syntax, from which indirect object syntax directly mirrors, as well as the rules for specifying a reference to be dereferenced.

However, the latter works; the former doesn't. We were getting no output. Finally, we enabled warnings (via -w on the command line)[*] and got this interesting series of messages:

```
Unquoted string "name" may clash with future reserved word at ./foo line 92.
Name "main::name" used only once: possible typo at ./foo line 92.
print() on unopened filehandle name at ./foo line 92.
```

Ahh, so that line was being parsed as:

```
print name ($cow, " eats.\n");
```

In other words, print the list of items to the filehandle named name. That's clearly not what we wanted, so we had to add additional syntax to disambiguate the call.

This leads us to our next strong suggestion:

Use direct object syntax at all times, except perhaps for the constructor call.

That exception acknowledges that most people write new Class ... rather than Class->new(...) and that most of us are fine with that. However, there are circumstances in which even that can lead to ambiguity (e.g., when a subroutine named new has been seen, and the class name itself has not been seen as a package). When in doubt, ignore indirect object syntax. Your maintenance programmer will thank you.

Additional Instance Variables in Subclasses

One of the nice things about using a hash for a data structure is that derived classes can add additional instance variables without the superclass needing to know of their addition. For example, let's derive a RaceHorse class that is everything a Horse is but also tracks its win/place/show/lose standings. The first part of this is trivial:

```
{ package RaceHorse;
  our @ISA = qw(Horse);
  ...
}
```

You'll also want to initialize "no wins of no races" when you create the RaceHorse. You do this by extending the named subroutine and adding four additional fields (wins, places, shows, losses, for first-, second-, and third-place finishes, and none of the above):

```
{ package RaceHorse;
  our @ISA = qw(Horse);
  ## extend parent constructor:
  sub named {
    my $self = shift->SUPER::named(@_);
    $self->{$_} = 0 for qw(wins places shows losses);
```

---

[*] Using -w should be the first step when Perl does something you don't understand. Or maybe it should be the zeroth because you should normally have -w in effect whenever you're developing code.

```
      $self;
    }
  }
```

Here, you pass all parameters to the superclass, which should return a fully formed Horse. However, because you pass RaceHorse as the class, it'd be already blessed into the RaceHorse class.[*] Next, add the four instance variables that go beyond those defined in the superclass, setting their initial values to 0. Finally, return the modified RaceHorse to the caller.

It's important to note here that we've actually "opened the box" a bit while writing this derived class. You know that the superclass uses a hash reference and that the superclass hierarchy doesn't use the four names chosen for a derived class. This is because RaceHorse will be a "friend" class (in C++ or Java terminology), accessing the instance variables directly. If the maintainer of Horse or Animal ever changes representation or names of variables, there could be a collision, which might go undetected except for that important day when you're showing off your code to the investors. Things get even more interesting if the hashref is changed to an arrayref as well.

One way to decouple this dependency is to use composition rather than inheritance as a way to create a derived class. In this example, you need to make a Horse object an instance variable of a RaceHorse and put the rest of the data in separate instance variables. You also need to pass any inherited method calls on the RaceHorse down to the Horse instance, through delegation. However, even though Perl can certainly support the needed operations, that approach is usually slower and more cumbersome. Enough on that for this discussion, however.

Next, let's provide some access methods:

```
{ package RaceHorse;
  our @ISA = qw(Horse);
  ## extend parent constructor:
  sub named {
    my $self = shift->SUPER::named(@_);
    $self->{$_} = 0 for qw(wins places shows losses);
    $self;
  }
  sub won { shift->{wins}++; }
  sub placed { shift->{places}++; }
  sub showed { shift->{shows}++; }
  sub lost { shift->{losses}++; }
  sub standings {
    my $self = shift;
    join ", ", map "$self->{$_} $_", qw(wins places shows losses);
  }
}
```

---

[*] Similar to the way the Animal constructor creates a Horse, not an Animal, when passed Horse as the class.

```
my $racer = RaceHorse->named("Billy Boy");
# record the outcomes: 3 wins, 1 show, 1 loss
$racer->won;
$racer->won;
$racer->won;
$racer->showed;
$racer->lost;
print $racer->name, " has standings of: ", $racer->standings, ".\n";
```

This prints:

```
Billy Boy has standings of: 3 wins, 0 places, 1 shows, 1 losses.
[Billy Boy has died.]
[Billy Boy has gone off to the glue factory.]
```

Note that we're still getting the Animal and Horse destructor. The superclasses are unaware that we've added four additional elements to the hash and so, still function as they always have.

Using Class Variables

What if you want to iterate over all the animals we've made so far? Animals may exist all over the program namespace and are lost once they're handed back from the named constructor method.

However, you can record the created animal in a hash and iterate over that hash. The key to the hash can be the stringified form of the animal reference,[*] while the value can be the actual reference, allowing you to access its name or class. For example, let's extend named as follows:

```
## in Animal
our %REGISTRY;
sub named {
  my $class = shift;
  my $name = shift;
  my $self = { Name => $name, Color => $class->default_color };
  bless $self, $class;
  $REGISTRY{$self} = $self;  # also returns $self
}
```

The uppercase name for %REGISTRY is a reminder that this variable is more global than most variables. In this case, it's a metavariable that contains information about many instances.

Note that when used as a key, $self *stringifies*, which means it turns into a string unique to the object.

---

[*] Or any other convenient and unique string.

We also need to add a new method:

```
sub registered {
  return map { "a ".ref($_)." named ".$_->name } values %REGISTRY;
}
```

Now you can see all the animals we've made:

```
my @cows = map Cow->named($_), qw(Bessie Gwen);
my @horses = map Horse->named($_), ("Trigger", "Mr. Ed");
my @racehorses = RaceHorse->named("Billy Boy");
print "We've seen:\n", map(" $_\n", Animal->registered);
print "End of program.\n";
```

This prints:

```
We've seen:
  a RaceHorse named Billy Boy
  a Horse named Mr. Ed
  a Horse named Trigger
  a Cow named Gwen
  a Cow named Bessie
End of program.
[Billy Boy has died.]
[Billy Boy has gone off to the glue factory.]
[Bessie has died.]
[Gwen has died.]
[Trigger has died.]
[Trigger has gone off to the glue factory.]
[Mr. Ed has died.]
[Mr. Ed has gone off to the glue factory.]
```

Note that the animals die at their proper time because the variables holding the animals are all being destroyed at the final step. Or are they?

Weakening the Argument

The %REGISTRY variable also holds a reference to each animal. So even if you toss away the containing variables:

```
{
  my @cows = map Cow->named($_), qw(Bessie Gwen);
  my @horses = map Horse->named($_), ("Trigger", "Mr. Ed");
  my @racehorses = RaceHorse->named("Billy Boy");
}
print "We've seen:\n", map(" $_\n", Animal->registered);
print "End of program.\n";
```

you'll still see the same result. The animals aren't destroyed even though none of the code is holding the animals. At first glance, it looks like you can fix this by altering the destructor:

```
## in Animal
sub DESTROY {
  my $self = shift;
```

```
      print "[", $self->name, " has died.]\n";
      delete $REGISTRY{$self};
   }
```

But this still results in the same output. Why? Because the destructor isn't called until the last reference is gone, but the last reference won't be destroyed until the destructor is called.*

One solution for fairly recent Perl versions† is to use weak references. A *weak* reference is a reference that doesn't count as far as the reference counting, uh, counts. It's best illustrated by example.

The weak reference mechanism is already built into the core of recent Perl versions, but as of this writing, the user interface is still accessed by a CPAN module called WeakRef. After installing this module,‡ you can update the constructor as follows:

```
## in Animal
use WeakRef qw(weaken); ## new

sub named {
  ref(my $class = shift) and croak "class only";
  my $name = shift;
  my $self = { Name => $name, Color => $class->default_color };
  bless $self, $class;
  $REGISTRY{$self} = $self;
  weaken($REGISTRY{$self});
  $self;
}
```

When Perl counts the number of active references to a thingy,§ it won't count any that have been converted to weak references by weaken. If all ordinary references are gone, Perl deletes the thingy and turns any weak references to undef.

Now you'll get the right behavior for:

```
my @horses = map Horse->named($_), ("Trigger", "Mr. Ed");
print "alive before block:\n", map(" $_\n", Animal->registered);
{
  my @cows = map Cow->named($_), qw(Bessie Gwen);
  my @racehorses = RaceHorse->named("Billy Boy");
  print "alive inside block:\n", map(" $_\n", Animal->registered);
}
print "alive after block:\n", map(" $_\n", Animal->registered);
print "End of program.\n";
```

---

* We'd make a reference to chickens and eggs, but that would introduce yet another derived class to Animal.

† 5.6 and later.

‡ See Chapter 15 for information on installing modules.

§ A *thingy* as defined in Perl's own documentation, is anything a reference points to, such as an object. If you are an especially boring person, you could call it a referent instead.

This prints:

```
alive before block:
  a Horse named Trigger
  a Horse named Mr. Ed
alive inside block:
  a RaceHorse named Billy Boy
  a Cow named Gwen
  a Horse named Trigger
  a Horse named Mr. Ed
  a Cow named Bessie
[Billy Boy has died.]
[Billy Boy has gone off to the glue factory.]
[Gwen has died.]
[Bessie has died.]
alive after block:
  a Horse named Trigger
  a Horse named Mr. Ed
End of program.
[Mr. Ed has died.]
[Mr. Ed has gone off to the glue factory.]
[Trigger has died.]
[Trigger has gone off to the glue factory.]
```

Notice that the racehorses and cows die at the end of the block, but the ordinary horses die at the end of the program. Success!

Weak references can also solve some memory leak issues. For example, suppose an animal wanted to record its pedigree. The parents might want to hold references to all their children while each child might want to hold references to each parent.

One or the other (or even both) of these links can be weakened. If the link to the child is weakened, the child can be destroyed when all other references are lost, and the parent's link simply becomes undef (or you can set a destructor to completely remove it). However, a parent won't disappear as long as it still has offspring. Similarly, if the link to the parent is weakened, you'll simply get it as undef when the parent is no longer referenced by other data structures. It's really quite flexible.*

Without weakening, as soon as any parent-child relationship is created, both the parent and the child remain in memory until the final global destruction phase, regardless of the destruction of the other structures holding either the parent or the child.

Be aware though: weak references should be used carefully, not just thrown at a problem of circular references. If you destroy data that is held by a weak reference before its time, you may have some very confusing programming problems to solve and debug.

---

* When using weak references, always make sure you don't dereference a weakened reference that has turned to undef.

Exercise

The answers for all exercises can be found in the Appendix.

Exercise [45 min]

Modify the RaceHorse class to get the previous standings from a DBM hash (keyed by the horse's name) when the horse is created, and update the standings when the horse is destroyed. For example, running this program four times:

```
my $runner = RaceHorse->named("Billy Boy");
$runner->won;
print $runner->name, " has standings ", $runner->standings, ".\n";
```

should show four additional wins. Make sure that a RaceHorse still does everything a normal Horse does otherwise.

For simplicity, use four space-separated integers for the value in the DBM hash.

CHAPTER 11

Some Advanced Object Topics

You might wonder, "do all objects inherit from a common class?" "What if a method is missing?" "What about multiple inheritance?" "How come we haven't seen a reference to a filehandle yet?" Well, wonder no more. This chapter covers these subjects and more.

UNIVERSAL Methods

As you define classes, you create inheritance hierarchies through the global @ISA variables in each package. To search for a method, Perl wanders through the @ISA tree until it finds a match or fails.

After the search fails however, Perl always looks in one special class called UNIVERSAL and invokes a method from there, if found, just as if it had been located in any other class or superclass.

One way to look at this is that UNIVERSAL is the base class from which all objects are derived. Any method you place here, such as:

```
sub UNIVERSAL::fandango {
  warn "object ", shift, " can do the fandango!\n";
}
```

enables all objects of your program to be called as $some_object->fandango.

Generally, you should provide a fandango method for specific classes of interest, and then provide a definition in UNIVERSAL::fandango as a backstop, in case a more specific method can't be found. A practical example might be a data-dumping routine for debugging or maybe a marshalling strategy to dump all application objects to a file. Simply provide the general method in UNIVERSAL and override it in the specific classes for unusual objects.

Obviously, UNIVERSAL should be used sparingly because there's only one universe of objects, and your fandango might collide with some other included module's fandango. For this reason, UNIVERSAL is hardly used for anything except methods which must be completely, well, universal. Like during debugging.

Testing Your Objects for Good Behavior

Besides providing a place for you to put universally available methods, the UNIVERSAL package comes preloaded with two very useful utility methods: isa and can. Because these methods are defined in UNIVERSAL, they are automatically available to all objects.

The isa method tests to see whether a given class or instance is a member of a given class or a member of a class that inherits from the given class. For example, continuing on with the Animal-family from the past chapters:

```
if (Horse->isa("Animal")) {    # does Horse inherit from Animal?
  print "A Horse is an Animal.\n";
}

my $tv_horse = Horse->named("Mr. Ed");
if ($tv_horse->isa("Animal")) { # is it an Animal?
  print $tv_horse->name, " is an Animal.\n";
  if ($tv_horse->isa("Horse")) { # is it a Horse?
    print "In fact, ", $tv_horse->name, " is a Horse.\n";
  } else {
    print "...but it's not a Horse.\n";
  }
}
```

This is handy when you have a heterogeneous mix of objects in a data structure and want to distinguish particular categories of objects:

```
my @horses = grep $_->isa("Horse"), @all_animals;
```

The result will be only the horses (or race horses) from the array. Compare that with:

```
my @horses_only = ref $_ eq "Horse", @all_animals;
```

which picks out *just* the horses because a RaceHorse won't return Horse for ref.

In general, you shouldn't use:

```
ref($some_object) eq "SomeClass"
```

in your programs because it prevents future users from subclassing that class. Use the isa construct as given earlier.

One downside of the isa call here is that it works only on blessed references or scalars that look like class names. If you happen to pass it an unblessed reference, you get a fatal (but trappable) error of:

```
Can't call method "isa" on unblessed reference at ...
```

To call isa more robustly, don't call it as a method. Instead, call it as a subroutine:

```
if (UNIVERSAL::isa($unknown_thing, "Animal")) {
  ... it's an Animal! ...
}
```

This works regardless of what $unknown_thing contains.

As in the case of isa, you can test for acceptable behaviors with the can method. For example:

```
if ($tv_horse->can("eat")) {
  $tv_horse->eat("hay");
}
```

If the result of can is true, then somewhere in the inheritance hierarchy, a class has defined an eat method. Again, the caveats about $tv_horse being only either a blessed reference or a class name as a scalar still apply, so the robust solution when you might deal with nearly anything looks like:

```
if (UNIVERSAL::can($tv_horse, "eat")) { ... }
```

Note that if you defined UNIVERSAL::fandango earlier, then:

```
$object->can("fandango")
```

always returns true because all objects can do the fandango.

AUTOLOAD as a Last Resort

After Perl searches the inheritance tree and UNIVERSAL for a method, it doesn't just stop there if the search is unsuccessful. Perl repeats the search through the very same hierarchy (including UNIVERSAL), looking for a method named AUTOLOAD.

If an AUTOLOAD exists, the subroutine is called in place of the original method, passing it the normal predetermined argument list: the class name or instance reference, followed by any arguments provided to the method call. The original method name is passed in the package variable called $AUTOLOAD (in the package where the subroutine was compiled) and contains the fully qualified method name, so you should generally strip everything up to the final double colon if you want a simple method name.

The AUTOLOAD subroutine can execute the desired operation itself, install a subroutine and then jump into it, or perhaps just die if asked to perform an unknown method.

One use of AUTOLOAD defers the compilation of a large subroutine until it is actually needed. For example, suppose the eat method for an animal is complex but unused in nearly every invocation of the program. You can defer its compilation as follows:

```
## in Animal
sub AUTOLOAD {
  our $AUTOLOAD;
```

```
  (my $method = $AUTOLOAD) =~ s/.*:://s; # remove package name
  if ($method eq "eat") {
    ## define eat:
    eval q{
      sub eat {
        ...
        long
        definition
        goes
        here
        ...
      }
    };                    # End of eval's q{} string
    die $@ if $@;                   # if typo snuck in
    goto &eat;                      # jump into it
  } else {                          # unknown method
    croak "$_[0] does not know how to $method\n";
  }
}
```

If the method name is eat, you'll define eat (which had previously been held in a string but not compiled), and then jump into it with a special construct that replaces the current subroutine invocation with an invocation to eat.* After the first AUTOLOAD hit, the eat subroutine is now defined, so won't be coming back here. This is great for compile-as-you-go programs because it minimizes startup overhead.

For a more automated way of creating code to do this, which makes it easy to turn the autoloading off during development and debugging, see the AutoLoader and SelfLoader core module documentation.

Using AUTOLOAD for Accessors

Chapter 9 showed how to create color and set_color to get and set the color of an animal. If you had 20 attributes instead of one or two, the code would be painfully repetitive. However, using an AUTOLOAD method, you can construct the nearly identical accessors as needed, saving both compilation time and wear-and-tear on the developer's keyboard.

Use a code reference as a closure to do the job. First, set up an AUTOLOAD for the object and define a list of hash keys for which you want trivial accessors:

```
sub AUTOLOAD {
  my @elements = qw(color age weight height);
```

Next, you'll see if the method is a getter for one of these keys, and if so, install a getter and jump to it:

---

* Although goto is generally (and rightfully) considered evil, this form of goto, which gives a subroutine name as a target, is not really the evil goto; it's the good goto.

```
  our $AUTOLOAD;
  if ($AUTOLOAD =~ /::(\w+)$/ and grep $1 eq $_, @elements) {
    my $field = ucfirst $1;
    {
      no strict 'refs';
      *{$AUTOLOAD} = sub { $_[0]->{$field} };
    }
    goto &{$AUTOLOAD};
  }
```

You need to use ucfirst because you named the method color to fetch the hash element called Color. The glob notation here installs a wanted subroutine as defined by the coderef closure, which fetches the corresponding key from the object hash. Consider this part to be magic that you just cut and paste into your program. Finally, the goto construct jumps into the newly defined subroutine.

Otherwise, perhaps it's a setter:

```
  if ($AUTOLOAD =~ /::set_(\w+)$/ and grep $1 eq $_, @elements) {
    my $field = ucfirst $1;
    {
      no strict 'refs';
      *{$AUTOLOAD} = sub { $_[0]->{$field} = $_[1] };
    }
    goto &{$AUTOLOAD};
  }
```

If it is neither, death awaits:

```
    die "$_[0] does not understand $method\n";
  }
```

Again, you pay the price for the AUTOLOAD only on the first hit of a particular getter or setter. After that, a subroutine is now already defined, and you can just invoke it directly.

Creating Getters and Setters More Easily

If all that coding for creating accessors using AUTOLOAD looks messy, rest assured that you really don't need to tackle it, because there's a CPAN module that does it a bit more directly: Class::MethodMaker.

For example, a simplified version of the Animal class might be defined as follows:

```
  package Animal;
  use Class::MethodMaker
    new_with_init => 'new',
    get_set => [-eiffel => [qw(color height name age)]],
    abstract => [qw(sound)],
  ;
  sub init {
    my $self = shift;
    $self->set_color($self->default_color);
```

```
}
sub named {
  my $self = shift->new;
  $self->set_name(shift);
  $self;
}
sub speak {
  my $self = shift;
  print $self->name, " goes ", $self->sound, "\n";
}
sub eat {
  my $self = shift;
  my $food = shift;
  print $self->name, " eats $food\n";
}
sub default_color {
  "brown";
}
```

The getters and setters for the four instance attributes (name, height, color, and age) are defined automatically, using the method color to get the color and set_color to set the color. (The eiffel flag says "do it the way the Eiffel language does it," which is the way it should be done here.) The messy blessing step is now hidden behind a simple new method. The initial color is defined as the default color, as before, because the init method is automatically called from new.

However, you can still call Horse->named('Mr. Ed') because it immediately calls the new routine as well.

The sound method is automatically generated as an abstract method. *Abstract* methods are placeholders, meant to be defined in a subclass. If a subclass fails to define the method, the method generated for Animal's sound dies.

You lose the ability to call the getters (such as name) on the class itself, rather than an instance. In turn, this breaks your prior usage of calling speak and eat on generic animals, since they call the accessors. One way around this is to define a more general version of name to handle either a class or instance and then change the other routines to call it:

```
sub generic_name {
  my $either = shift;
  ref $either ? $either->name : "an unnamed $either";
}
sub speak {
  my $either = shift;
  print $either->generic_name, " goes ", $either->sound, "\n";
}
sub eat {
  my $either = shift;
  my $food = shift;
  print $either->generic_name, " eats $food\n";
}
```

There. Now it's looking nearly drop-in compatible with the previous definition, except for those friend classes that referenced the attribute names directly in the hash as the initial-cap-keyed versions (such as Color) rather than through the accessors ($self->color).

That brings up the maintenance issue again. The more you can decouple your implementation (hash versus array, names of hash keys, or types of elements) from the interface (method names, parameter lists, or types of return values), the more flexible and maintainable your system becomes.

That flexibility is not free, however. The cost of a method call is higher than the cost of a hash lookup, so it may be acceptable (or even necessary) for a friend class to peer inside. You may have to pay the programmer-time price of development and maintenance so you don't pay the runtime price of an overly flexible system.

On the other hand, don't go overboard in the other direction. Many anecdotes float around about systems where everything was so indirected (to be flexible) that the system ran too slowly to be used.

Multiple Inheritance

How does Perl wander through the @ISA tree? The answer may be simple or complex. If you don't have multiple inheritance (that is, if no @ISA has more than one element), it is simple: Perl simply goes from one @ISA to the next until it finds the ultimate base class whose @ISA is empty.

Multiple inheritance is more complex. It occurs when a class's @ISA has more than one element. For example, suppose someone had given an existing class, called Racer, which has the basic abilities for anything that can race, so that it's ready to be the base class for a runner, a fast car, or a racing turtle. With that, you can make the RaceHorse class as simply as this, maybe:[*]

```
{
  package RaceHorse;
  our @ISA = qw{ Horse Racer };
}
```

Now a RaceHorse can do anything a Horse can do, and anything a Racer can do as well. When Perl searches for a method that's not provided directly by RaceHorse, it first searches through all the capabilities of the Horse (including all its parent classes, such as Animal). When the Horse possibilities are exhausted, Perl turns to see whether Racer (or one of its subclasses) supplies the needed method. On the other hand, if

---

[*] If there is a conflict among the methods of Horse and Racer, or if their implementations aren't able to work together, the situation can become much more difficult.

you want Perl to search Racer and its subclasses before searching Horse, put them into @ISA in that order (see Figure 11-1).

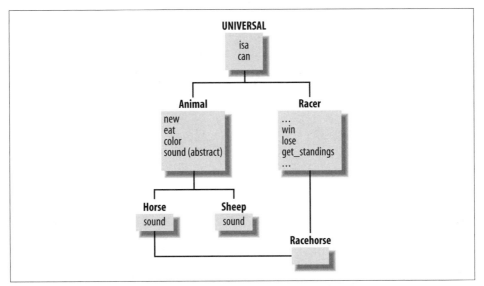

Figure 11-1. A class may not need to implement any methods of its own if it inherits everything it needs from its parent classes through multiple inheritance

References to Filehandles

So far, you've seen references to scalars, arrays, hashes, and subroutines. Another important value type in Perl is the *filehandle*.

However, a filehandle isn't stored in a variable. The filehandle is the handle itself. You can't take a reference directly to a filehandle.* However, using the IO::File built-in class, you can create objects that act like filehandles within Perl. Here's a typical use:

```
use IO::File;

my $fh = IO::File->open("/etc/passwd")
  or die "constructor failed: $!";

while (<$fh>) {          # $fh acts like any filehandle
  print "a password line is $_";
}

close $fh;              # nearly all built-ins can use IO::File
```

---

* You can use the glob, take a reference to the glob, or take a reference to the I/O structure within a glob, but that's still not a reference to the filehandle.

Here, $fh is constructed using the open class method of IO::File, and then used in places where ordinarily you'd use a traditional (bareword) filehandle. Furthermore, you also get some additional methods:

```
if ($fh->opened) { ... } # file is open

$fh->blocking(0);        # make I/O be "non-blocking" if supported
```

The core built-in operations that use filehandles can all use an IO::File objects instead. If the IO::File object is within a simple scalar variable, you can always replace the filehandle with the scalar:

```
use IO::File;
my $fh = IO::File->new; # create unopened "filehandle" object

open $fh, ">my_new_file" or die "Cannot create: $!";
print $fh "$_\n" for 1..10;
close $fh;
```

An IO::File object automatically gets closed cleanly when destroyed, so you can simplify the previous code as:

```
use IO::File;
{
  my $fh = IO::File->open(">my_new_file")
    or die "Cannot create my_new_file: $!";
  print $fh, "$_\n" for 1..10;
}
```

As $fh goes out of scope, the filehandle is automatically closed. Nice.

If the IO::File object is not named by a simple scalar variable, some operations require a slightly modified syntax to work. For example, copy every file matched by the glob pattern of *.input to a corresponding file whose suffix is .output, but do it in parallel. First, open all the files, both inputs and outputs:

```
my @handlepairs;
foreach my $file (<*.input>) {
  (my $out = $file) =~ s/\.input$/.output/;
  push @handlepairs, [
    (IO::File->new("<$file") || die),
    (IO::File->new(">$out") || die),
  ];
}
```

Now you have an array of references to arrays, each element of which is an IO::File object. Let's pump the data:

```
while (@handlepairs) {
  @handlepairs = grep {
    if (defined(my $line = $_->[0]->getline)) {
      print { $_->[1] } $line;
    } else {
      0;
```

```
      }
    } @handlepairs;
  }
```

As long as you have pairs, keep passing the list through the grep structure:

```
@handlepairs = grep { CONDITION } @handlepairs;
```

On each pass, only the handle pairs that evaluate as true in the grep CONDITION sur-vive. Inside, you take the first element of each pair and try to read from it. If that's successful, write that line to the second element of the pair (the corresponding out-put handle). If the print is successful, it returns true, which lets grep know that you want to keep that pair. If either the print fails or the getline returned undef, the grep sees the false value as an indication to discard that pair. Discarding the pair automat-ically closes both filehandles. Cool!

Note that you can't use the more traditional filehandle read or filehandle print opera-tions because the reading and writing filehandles weren't in a simple scalar variable. Rewrite that loop to see if copying the handles is easier:

```
while (@handlepairs) {
  @handlepairs = grep {
    my ($IN, $OUT) = @$_;
    if (defined(my $line = <$IN>)) {
      print $OUT $line;
    } else {
      0;
    }
  } @handlepairs;
}
```

This scenario is arguably better. Most of the time, simply copying the complexly ref-erenced value into a simple scalar is easier on the eyes. In fact, another way to write that loop is to get rid of the ugly if structure:

```
while (@handlepairs) {
  @handlepairs = grep {
    my ($IN, $OUT) = @$_;
    my $line;
    defined($line = <IN>) and print $OUT $line;
  } @handlepairs;
}
```

As long as someone understands that and is a partial evaluator and that print returns true when everything is OK, this is a fine replacement. Remember the Perl motto: "There's more than one way to do it" (although not all of them are equally nice or legitimate).

Exercise

The answers for all exercises can be found in the Appendix.

Exercise [30 min]

The Professor has to read a log file that looks like:

```
Gilligan: 1 coconut
Skipper: 3 coconuts
Gilligan: 1 banana
Ginger: 2 papayas
Professor: 3 coconuts
MaryAnn: 2 papayas
...
```

He wants to write a series of files, called `gilligan.info`, `maryann.info`, and so on. Each file should contain all the lines that begin with that name. (Names are always delimited by the trailing colon.) At the end, `gilligan.info` should start with:

```
Gilligan: 1 coconut
Gilligan: 1 banana
```

Now the log file is large, and the coconut-powered computer is not very fast, so he wants to process the input file in one pass and write all output files in parallel. How does he do it?

Hint: Use a hash, keyed by the castaway name, holding `IO::File` objects for each output file. Create them as necessary.

## CHAPTER 12

Using Modules

A module is a building block for your program: a set of related subroutines and variables packaged so it can be reused. This chapter looks at the basics of modules: how to bring in modules that others have written, and how to write modules of your own.

Sample Function-Oriented Interface: File::Basename

To understand what happens with use, look at one of the many modules included with a normal Perl distribution: File::Basename. This module parses file specifications into useful pieces in a mostly portable manner. The default usage:

```
use File::Basename;
```

introduces three subroutines, fileparse, basename, and dirname,* into the current package: typically, main in the main part of your program. From this point forward, within this package, you can say: †

```
my $basename = basename($some_full_path);
my $dirname = dirname($some_full_path);
```

as if you had written the basename and dirname subroutines yourself, or (nearly) as if they were built-in Perl functions.‡

However, suppose you already had a dirname subroutine? You've now overwritten it with the definition provided by File::Basename! If you had turned on warnings, you'd see a message stating that, but otherwise, Perl really doesn't care.

---

* As well as a utility routine, fileparse_set_fstype.

† The new symbols are available for all code compiled in the current package from this point on, whether it's in this same file or not. However, these symbols won't be available in a different package.

‡ These routines pick out the filename and the directory parts of a pathname. For example, if $some_full_path were D:\Projects\Island Rescue\plan 7.rtf (presumably, the program is running on a Windows machine), the *basename* would be plan 7.rtf and the *dirname* would be D:\Projects\Island Rescue.

Selecting What to Import

Fortunately, you can tell the use operation to limit its actions. Do this by specifying a list of subroutine names following the module name, called the *import list*:

```
use File::Basename ("fileparse", "basename");
```

Now define the two given subroutines from the module, leaving your own `dirname` alone. Of course, this is awkward to type, so more often you'll see this written as:

```
use File::Basename qw( fileparse basename );
```

In fact, even if there's only one item, you tend to write it with a qw( ) list for consistency and maintenance; often you'll go back to say "give me another one from here," and it's simpler if it's already a qw( ) list.

You've protected the local `dirname` routine, but what if you still want the functionality provided by `File::Basename`'s `dirname`? No problem. Just spell it out in full:

```
my $dirname = File::Basename::dirname($some_path);
```

The list of names following use doesn't change which subroutine is defined in the module's package (in this case, `File::Basename`). You can always use the full name regardless of the import list, as in:[*]

```
my $basename = File::Basename::basename($some_path);
```

In an extreme (but extremely useful) case, you can specify an empty list for the import list, as in:

```
use File::Basename ();              # no import
my $base = File::Basename::basename($some_path);
```

An empty list is different from an absent list. An empty list says "don't give me anything in my current package," while an absent list says "give me the defaults."[†] If the module's author has done her job well, the default will probably be exactly what you want.

Sample Object-Oriented Interface: File::Spec

Contrast the subroutines imported by `File::Basename` with what another core (non-CPAN) module has by looking at `File::Spec`. The `File::Spec` module is designed to support operations commonly performed on file specifications. (A file specification is usually a file or directory name, but it may be a name of a file that doesn't exist—in which case, it's not really a filename, is it?)

---

[*] You don't need the ampersand in front of any of these subroutine invocations because the subroutine name is already known to the compiler following use.

[†] As you'll see later in this chapter, the default list comes from the module's @EXPORT array.

Unlike the File::Basename module, the File::Spec module has a primarily object-oriented interface. Saying:

```
use File::Spec;
```

in your program imports no subroutines into the current package. Instead, you're expected to access the functionality of the module using class methods:

```
my $filespec = File::Spec->catfile( $homedir{gilligan},
    'web_docs', 'photos', 'USS_Minnow.gif' );
```

This calls the class method catfile of the File::Spec class, building a path appropriate for the local operating system, and returns a single string.* This is similar in syntax to the nearly two dozen other operations provided by File::Spec: they're all called as class methods. No instances are ever created.

While it is never stated in the documentation, perhaps the purpose of creating these as class methods rather than as imported subroutines is to free the user of the module from having to worry about namespace collisions (as you saw for dirname in the previous section). The idea of an object class without objects, however, seems a bit off kilter. Perhaps, that's why the module's author also provides a more traditional interface with:

```
use File::Spec::Functions qw(catfile curdir);
```

in which two of the File::Spec's many functions are imported as ordinary callable subroutines:

```
my $filespec = catfile( $homedir{gilligan},
    'web_docs', 'photos', 'USS_Minnow.gif' );
```

A More Typical Object-Oriented Module: Math::BigInt

So as not to get dismayed about how "un-OO" the File::Spec module might be, let's look at yet another core module, Math::BigInt:

```
use Math::BigInt;
my $value = Math::BigInt->new(2); # start with 2
$value->bpow(1000);               # take 2**1000
print $value->bstr( ), "\n";      # print it out
```

Here, nothing is imported. The entire interface calls class methods such as new against the class name to create instances, and then calls instance methods against those instances.

---

* That string might be something like /home/gilligan/web_docs/photos/USS_Minnow.gif on a Unix system. On a Windows system, it would typically use backslashes as directory separators. As you can see, this module lets you write portable code easily, at least where file specs are concerned.

The Differences Between OO and Non-OO Modules

A primarily OO module is distinguished from a primarily non-OO module in two ways:

- A *primarily OO* module has functions that are meant to be called as a class methods, possibly returning instances upon which you issue further instance method calls.

- A *primarily non-OO* module generally doesn't export any functions at all, making the import list rather irrelevant.

Because methods of the OO module are meant to be called as class methods, they should all set aside their first argument, which is the class name. This class name blesses a new instance but is otherwise ignored. Thus, you should not call OO modules as if they were functional modules, and vice versa. Stick with the design of the module.

What use Is Doing

So, just what is that use doing? How does the import list come in to action? Perl interprets the use list as a particular form of BEGIN block wrapped around a require and a method call. For example, the following two operations are equivalent:

```
use Island::Plotting::Maps qw( load_map scale_map draw_map );

BEGIN {
  require Island::Plotting::Maps;
  Island::Plotting::Maps->import( qw( load_map scale_map draw_map ) );
}
```

Break this code down piece by piece. First, the require. This require is a package-name require, rather than the string-expression require from earlier chapters. The colons are turned into the native directory separator (such as / for Unix-like systems), and the name is suffixed with .pm (for "perl module"). For this example on a Unix-like system, you end up with:

```
require "Island/Plotting/Maps.pm";
```

Recalling the operation of require from earlier, this means you look in the current value of @INC, checking through each directory for a subdirectory named Island that contains a further subdirectory named Plotting that contains the file named Maps.pm.*

---

* The .pm portion is defined by the interface and can't be changed. Thus, all module filenames must end in dot-p-m.

If an appropriate file isn't found after looking at all of @INC, the program dies.* Otherwise, the first file found is read and evaluated. As always with require, the last expression evaluated must be true (or the program dies),† and once a file has been read, it will not be reread if requested again.‡

In the module interface, the require'd file is expected to define subroutines in the same-named package, not the caller's package. So, for example, a portion of the File::Basename file might look something like this, if you took out all the good stuff:

```
package File::Basename;
sub dirname { ... }
sub basename { ... }
sub fileparse { ... }
1;
```

These three subroutines are then defined in the File::Basename package, not the package in which the use occurs. A require'd file must return a true value, so it's traditional to use 1; as the last line of a module's code.

How are these subroutines imported from the module's package to the user's package? That's the second step inside the BEGIN block. A routine called import in the module's package is called, passing along the entire import list. The module author is responsible for providing an appropriate import routine. It's easier than it sounds, as discussed later in this chapter.

Finally, the whole thing is wrapped in a BEGIN block. This implies that the use operation happens at compile time, rather than runtime, and indeed it does. Thus, subroutines are associated with those defined in the module, prototypes are properly defined, and so on.

Setting the Path at the Right Time

The downside of use being executed at compile time is that it also looks at @INC at compile time, which can break your program in hard-to-understand ways unless you take @INC into consideration.

For example, suppose you have your own directory under /home/gilligan/lib, and you place your own Navigation::SeatOfPants module in /home/gilligan/lib/Navigation/SeatOfPants.pm. Simply saying:

```
use Navigation::SeatOfPants;
```

---

* Trappable with an eval, of course.

† Again trappable with eval.

‡ Thanks to the %INC hash.

is unlikely to do anything useful because only the system directories (and typically the current directory) are considered for @INC. However, even adding:

```
push @INC, "/home/gilligan/lib";   # broken
use Navigation::SeatOfPants;
```

doesn't work. Why? Because the push happens at runtime, long after the use was attempted at compile time. One way to fix this is to add a BEGIN block around the push:

```
BEGIN { push @INC, "/home/gilligan/lib"; }
use Navigation::SeatOfPants;
```

Now the BEGIN block compiles and executes at compile time, setting up the proper path for the following use.

However, this is noisy and prone to require far more explanation than you might be comfortable with, especially for the maintenance programmer who has to edit your code later. Let's replace all that clutter with a simple pragma:

```
use lib "/home/gilligan/lib";
use Navigation::SeatOfPants;
```

Here, the lib pragma takes one or more arguments and adds them at the beginning of the @INC array (think "unshift").* It does so because it is processed at compile time, not runtime. Hence, it's ready in time for the use immediately following.

Because a use lib pragma will pretty much always have a site-dependent pathname, it is traditional and encouraged to put it near the top of the file. This makes it easier to find and update when the file needs to move to a new system or when the lib directory's name changes. (Of course, you can eliminate use lib entirely if you can install your modules in a standard @INC locations, but that's not always practical.)

Think of use lib as not "use this library," but rather "use this path to find my libraries (and modules)." Too often, you see code written like:

```
use lib "/home/gilligan/lib/Navigation/SeatOfPants.pm"; # WRONG
```

and then the programmer wonders why it didn't pull in the definitions. Be aware that use lib indeed runs at compile time, so this also doesn't work:

```
my $LIB_DIR = "/home/gilligan/lib";
...
use lib $LIB_DIR;     # BROKEN
use Navigation::SeatOfPants;
```

Certainly the declaration of $LIB_DIR is established at compile time (so you won't get an error with use strict, although the actual use lib should complain), but the

---

* use lib also unshifts an architecture-dependent library below the requested library, making it more valuable than the explicit counterpart presented earlier.

actual initialization to the /home/gilligan/lib/ path happens at runtime. Oops, too late again!

At this point, you need to put something inside a BEGIN block or perhaps rely on yet another compile-time operation: setting a constant with use constant:

```
use constant LIB_DIR => "/home/gilligan/lib";
...
use lib LIB_DIR;
use Navigation::SeatOfPants;
```

There. Fixed again. That is, until you need the library to depend on the result of a calculation. (Where will it all end? Somebody stop the madness!) This should handle about 99 percent of your needs.

Importing with Exporter

Earlier we skipped over that "and now magic happens" part where the import routine (defined by the module author) is supposed to take File::Basename::fileparse and somehow alias it into the caller's package so it's callable as fileparse.

Perl provides a lot of introspection capabilities. Specifically, you can look at the symbol table (where all subroutines and most variables are named), see what is defined, and alter those definitions. You saw a bit of that back in the AUTOLOAD mechanism earlier. In fact, as the author of File::Basename, if you simply want to force filename, basename, and fileparse from the current package into the main package, you can write import like this:

```
sub import {
  no strict 'refs';
  for (qw(filename basename fileparse)) {
    *{"main::$_"} = \&$_;
  }
}
```

Boy, is that cryptic! And limited. What if you didn't want fileparse? What if you invoked use in a package other than main?

Thankfully, there's a standard import that's available in the Exporter module. As the module author, all you do is add:

```
use Exporter;
our @ISA = qw(Exporter);
```

Now the import call to the package will inherit upward to the Exporter class, providing an import routine that knows how to take a list of subroutines* and export them to the caller's package.

---

* And variables, although far less common, and arguably the wrong thing to do.

@EXPORT and @EXPORT_OK

The `import` provided by Exporter examines the `@EXPORT` variable in the module's package to determine which variables are exported by default. For example, `File::Basename` might do something like:

```
package File::Basename;
our @EXPORT = qw( basename dirname fileparse );
use Exporter;
our @ISA = qw(Exporter);
```

The `@EXPORT` list both defines a list of available subroutines for export (the public interface) and provides a default list to be used when no import list is specified. For example, these two calls are equivalent:

```
use File::Basename;
```

```
BEGIN { require File::Basename; File::Basename->import }
```

No list is passed to `import`. In that case, the `Exporter->import` routine looks at `@EXPORT` and provides everything in the list.[*]

What if you had subroutines you didn't want as part of the default import but would still be available if requested? You can add those subroutines to the `@EXPORT_OK` list in the module's package. For example, suppose that Gilligan's module provides the `guess_direction_toward` routine by default but could also provide the `ask_the_skipper_about` and `get_north_from_professor` routines, if requested. You can start it like this:

```
package Navigate::SeatOfPants;
our @EXPORT = qw(guess_direction_toward);
our @EXPORT_OK = qw(ask_the_skipper_about get_north_from_professor);
use Exporter;
our @ISA = qw(Exporter);
```

The following invocations would then be valid:

```
use Navigate::SeatOfPants;  # gets guess_direction_toward
```

```
use Navigate::SeatOfPants qw(guess_direction_toward); # same
```

```
use Navigate::SeatOfPants
  qw(guess_direction_toward ask_the_skipper_about);
```

```
use Navigate::SeatOfPants
  qw(ask_the_skipper_about get_north_from_professor);
  ## does NOT import guess_direction_toward!
```

---

[*] Remember, having no list is not the same as having an empty list. If the list is empty, the module's `import` method is simply not called at all.

If any names are specified, they must come from either @EXPORT or @EXPORT_OK, so this request is rejected by Exporter->import:

```
use Navigate::SeatOfPants qw(according_to_GPS);
```

because according_to_GPS is in neither @EXPORT nor @EXPORT_OK.* Thus, with those two arrays, you have control over your public interface. This does not stop someone from saying Navigate::SeatOfPants::according_to_GPS (if it existed), but at least now it's obvious that they're using something the module author didn't intend to offer them.

As described in the Exporter manpage, a few shortcuts are available automatically. You can provide a list that is the same as asking for the default:

```
use Navigate::SeatOfPants qw(:DEFAULT);
```

or the default plus some others:

```
use Navigate::SeatOfPants qw(:DEFAULT get_north_from_professor);
```

These are rarely seen in practice. Why? The purpose of explicitly providing an import list generally means you want to control the subroutine names you use in your program. Those last examples do not insulate you from future changes to the module, which may import additional subroutines that could collide with your code.†

In a few cases, a module may supply dozens or hundreds of possible symbols. These modules can use advanced techniques (described in the Exporter documentation) to make it easy to import batches of related symbols. For example, the core Fcntl module makes the flock constants available as a group with the :flock tag:

```
use Fcntl qw( :flock );        # import all flock constants
```

Exporting in a Primarily OO Module

As seen earlier, the normal means of using an object-oriented module is to call class methods and then methods against instances resulting from constructors of that class. This means that an OO module typically exports nothing, so you'll have:

```
package My::OOModule::Base;
our @EXPORT = ( ); # you may even omit this line
use Exporter;
our @ISA = qw(Exporter);
```

As stated in Chapter 8, you can even shorten this down:

```
package My::OOModule::Base;
use base qw(Exporter);
```

---

* This check also catches misspellings and mistaken subroutine names, keeping you from wondering why the get_direction_from_professor routine isn't working.

† For this reason, it is generally considered a bad idea for an update to a released module to introduce new default imports. If you know that your first release is still missing a function, though, there's no reason why you can't put in a placeholder: sub according_to_GPS { die "not implemented yet" }.

What if you then derive a class from this base class? The most important thing to remember is that the import method must be defined from the Exporter class, so you add it like so:

```
package My::OOModule::Derived;
use base qw(Exporter My::OOModule::Base);
```

However, wouldn't the call to My::OOModule::Derived->import eventually find its way up to Exporter via My::OOModule::Base? Sure it would. So you can leave that out:

```
package My::OOModule::Derived;
use base qw(My::OOModule::Base);
```

Only the base classes at the top of the tree need specify Exporter and only when they derive from no other classes.

Please be aware of all the other reserved method names that can't be used by your OO module (as described in the Exporter manpage). At the time of this writing, the list is export_to_level, require_version, and export_fail. Also, you may wish to reserve unimport because that routine will be called by replacing use with no. That use is rare for user-written modules, however.

Even though an OO module typically exports nothing, you might choose to export a named constructor or management routine. This routine typically acts a bit like a class method but is meant to be called as a normal routine.

One example can be found in the LWP library (on the CPAN). The URI::URL module (now deprecated and replaced by the URI module) deals with universal resource identifiers, most commonly seen as URLs such as *http://www.gilligan.crew.hut/maps/island.pdf*. You can construct a URI::URL object as a traditional object constructor with:

```
use URI::URL;
my $u = URI::URL->new("http://www.gilligan.crew.hut/maps/island.pdf");
```

The default import list for URI::URL also imports a url subroutine, which can be used as a constructor as well:

```
use URI::URL;
my $u = url("http://www.gilligan.crew.hut/maps/island.pdf");
```

Because this imported routine isn't a class method, you don't use the arrow method call to invoke it. Also, the routine is unlike anything else in the module: no initial class parameter is passed. Even though normal subroutines and method calls are both defined as subroutines in the package, the caller and the author must agree as to which is which.

The url convenience routine was nice, initially. However, it also clashed with the same-name routine in CGI.pm, leading to interesting errors (especially in a mod_perl setting). (The modern interface in the URI module doesn't export such a constructor.) Prior to that, in order to prevent a crash, you had to remember to bring it in as:

```
use URI::URL ();          # don't import "url"
my $u = URI::URL->new(...);
```

Custom Import Routines

Let's use CGI.pm as an example of a custom import routine. Not satisfied with the incredible flexibility of the Exporter's import routine, author Lincoln Stein created a special import for the CGI module.* If you've ever gawked at the dizzying array of options that can appear after use CGI, it's all a simple matter of programming.

As part of the extension provided by this custom import, you can use the CGI module as an object-oriented module:

```
use CGI;
my $q = CGI->new;          # create a query object
my $f = $q->param("foo");  # get the foo field
```

or a function-oriented module:

```
use CGI qw(param);          # import the param function
my $f = param("foo");       # get the foo field
```

If you don't want to spell out every possible subfunction, bring them all in:

```
use CGI qw(:all);          # define "param" and 800-gazillion others
my $f = param("foo");
```

And then there's pragmata available. For example, if you want to disable the normal sticky field handling, simply add -nosticky into the import list:

```
use CGI qw(-nosticky :all);
```

If you want to create the start_table and end_table routines, in addition to the others, it's simply:

```
use CGI qw(-nosticky :all *table);
```

Truly a dizzying array of options.

Exercise

The answers for all exercises can be found in the Appendix.

Exercise [15 min]

Take the library you created in Chapter 2 and turn it into a module you can bring in with use. Alter the invoking code so that it uses the imported routines (rather than the full path), and test it.

---

* Some have dubbed this the "Lincoln Loader" out of simultaneous deep respect for Lincoln and the sheer terror of having to deal with something that just doesn't work like anything else they've encountered.

CHAPTER 13
Writing a Distribution

In Chapter 12, you created a fictional Island::Plotting::Maps module, and built the right support for Exporter so that you could include use Island::Plotting::Maps in a program.

While the resulting .pm file is useful, it's not very practical. There's a lot more to building a real module than just creating the .pm file. You'll also need to consider and implement the following questions:

Installation location
> How and where is the .pm file installed so a program can find the module in its @INC path?

Documentation
> Where is the documentation for the module? How is the documentation installed so the user can read it?

Archive completeness
> If there are any accompanying files, where are they? How can the end user know if any missing files are missing?

Testing
> What test harnesses can the developer run to verify correct operation, including testing against older known bugs? Can these same tests be run by the installer to ensure proper operation in the target environment?

C-language interfaces
> If the module contains C or C++ code (not covered here), how can the developer describe how to compile and link the code in the developer's environment, or the end user environment?

As Roy Scheider uttered in the movie *Jaws*: "You're gonna need a bigger boat." That "bigger boat" is the difference between a module and a distribution.

Starting with h2xs

A distribution contains the module (or collection of related modules), plus all the support files required to document, test, ship, and install the module. While you could potentially construct all these files by hand, it's much simpler to use a tool that comes with Perl, awkwardly called h2xs[*]

The h2xs tool creates a series of template files that serve as a starting point for the distribution files. You simply need to say h2xs -XAn, followed by the name of the module—in this case, Island::Plotting::Maps.[†] Here's what the output looks like:[‡]

```
$ h2xs -XAn Island::Plotting::Maps
Defaulting to backwards compatibility with perl 5.8.0
If you intend this module to be compatible with earlier perl versions, please
specify a minimum perl version with the -b option.

Writing Island/Plotting/Maps/Maps.pm
Writing Island/Plotting/Maps/Makefile.PL
Writing Island/Plotting/Maps/README
Writing Island/Plotting/Maps/t/1.t
Writing Island/Plotting/Maps/Changes
Writing Island/Plotting/Maps/MANIFEST
```

Looking at the Templates

You'll create some subdirectories below the current directory and a bunch of files in the lowest of those directories. Let's look at them to see what they are. First, cd into the directory:

```
$ cd Island/Plotting/Maps
```

Now, let's examine the MANIFEST file:

```
$ cat MANIFEST
Changes
Makefile.PL
MANIFEST
Maps.pm
README
t/1.t
```

---

[*] The name h2xs has an interesting pedigree. Back in the early days of Perl 5, Larry invented the XS language to describe the glue code that Perl needs to talk to C-language functions and libraries. Originally, this code was written entirely by hand, but the h2xs tool was written to scan simple C-include header files (ending in .h) and generate most of the XS directly. Hence, h "2" (to) XS. Over time, more functions were added, including generating template files for the rest of the distribution. Now here we are, about to describe how to use h2xs for things that aren't either h or xs. Amazing.

[†] If there's more than one module in the distribution, it should be the name of the most important module. Others can be added later.

[‡] The exact behavior and output of h2xs may vary depending upon your version of Perl.

The MANIFEST file resembles a table of contents for the distribution. When you eventually bundle up everything and ship it off to the CPAN or the ultimate recipient, the bundling tool looks at MANIFEST to know what to include, and the unpacking tool verifies that everything in MANIFEST is present at the destination. Of course, MANIFEST lists MANIFEST, but it also lists everything else created by h2xs automatically.

While maintaining a MANIFEST sounds like it might be painful, you can be assured that you won't accidentally include your "notes to self" in the distribution just because the file happened to be in the wrong directory. Specific steps discussed later keep the MANIFEST up to date.

The next, mostly uninteresting, file is README, which is self-describing:

```
$ cat README
Island/Plotting/Maps version 0.01
= == == == == == == == == == == == == == == ==

The README is used to introduce the module and provide instructions on
how to install the module, any machine dependencies it may have (for
example C compilers and installed libraries) and any other information
that should be provided before the module is installed.

A README file is required for CPAN modules since CPAN extracts the
README file from a module distribution so that people browsing the
archive can use it get an idea of the modules uses. It is usually a
good idea to provide version information here so that people can
decide whether fixes for the module are worth downloading.

INSTALLATION

To install this module type the following:

   perl Makefile.PL
   make
   make test
   make install

DEPENDENCIES

This module requires these other modules and libraries:

  blah blah blah

COPYRIGHT AND LICENCE

Put the correct copyright and licence information here.

Copyright (C) 2002 Ginger Grant

This library is free software; you can redistribute it and/or modify
it under the same terms as Perl itself.
```

Obviously, you will want to edit this file to be whatever you want it to be. The phrase "blah blah blah" is often used in the templates to indicate things that must be changed.* If you leave unchanged the blah blah blah and other notes from h2xs to you, potential users will suspect that bugs in the code have also escaped your scrutiny, so proofread this stuff (and your code) before you distribute your module.

Pay special attention to the copyright and license section. (It should have your name in place of Ginger's name, unless your machine is very confused about who is sitting at the keyboard.) Your employer may require you to change the copyright notice to include your company name rather than your name, for example. Or, if you're including someone else's code in your module, you may need to mention their copyright (or lack thereof) as well.

The README file also has a special responsibility: the master CPAN archiving tools pull out the README file as a separate entry automatically, permitting the file to be indexed by search engines on the various worldwide archives, and to be downloaded and read trivially by the CPAN installation tools. In the CPAN.pm shell, for example, you can say:†

```
$ perl -MCPAN -eshell
cpan> readme Island::Plotting::Maps
```

and the contents of the README file will be shown without having to download and unpack the entire distribution.

Another file created as a template is Changes:

```
$ cat Changes
Revision history for Perl extension Island::Plotting::Maps.

0.01  Wed Oct 16 15:53:23 2002
        - original version; created by h2xs 1.22 with options
            -XAn Island::Plotting::Maps
```

You'll need to maintain this file manually, unless your interactive development environment has automated tools for such maintenance. Most people will expect to be able to look here to see what has been updated in new releases of your module. Try not to disappoint them. One of the main purposes of the Changes file is debugging: if you realize that a certain bug turned up three releases back, you can look here to remind yourself of new features or bug fixes that were introduced in that release.

---

* When you're bored, you might find it amusing to do a search of the current CPAN for all places in which blah blah blah occurs.

† Well, you *would* be able to do this, if there were actually a module on CPAN named Island::Plotting::Maps.

The Prototype Module Itself

Now you come to the most important part of the distribution: the module itself. Finally, actual code:

```
$ cat Maps.pm
package Island::Plotting::Maps;
```

It looks good so far. The module automatically starts with an appropriate package directive. Following that, you see:

```
use 5.008;
use strict;
use warnings;
```

Now you're declaring that the module is compatible with Perl 5.8.0 or later and that the compiler restrictions and warnings are enabled automatically. Good practices are encouraged here. Obviously, you're free to delete or modify anything inappropriate.

Then comes Exporter:

```
require Exporter;

our @ISA = qw(Exporter);
```

These lines support the import method call needed to make use work. This is fine for a nonobject-oriented module, but for an object-oriented module inheriting from a parent (base) class, you'll want to replace them with:

```
use base qw(Our::Parent::Class);
```

Resulting in more Exporter control:

```
our %EXPORT_TAGS = ( 'all' => [ qw(

) ] );

our @EXPORT_OK = ( @{ $EXPORT_TAGS{'all'} } );

our @EXPORT = qw(

);
```

Every symbol you wish to possibly import as a result of the use operation should be placed into the first qw( ) list. This lets you say:

```
use OurModule qw(:all)
```

to get all possible symbols.*

---

* Technically, you don't need :all because /^/ (include all symbols that match at least a beginning of string) does the same. Many people are familiar with typing :all, and it's far more self-documenting than /^/ is, so include it if you can.

Every symbol you wish to export *by default* on a missing import list should go into the last qw( ). (Any symbol in the @EXPORT list is automatically a member of the @EXPORT_OK list, but you'll want to list it again it the first qw( ) list so it comes in via the :all method.)

Recall from Chapter 12 that a typical object-oriented module exports nothing because the interface is entirely through class method calls and instance method calls, neither of which require subroutines in the invoker's package.

Next, you'll see the version number:

```
our $VERSION = '0.01';
```

This version number is important for many reasons:

Unique identification
> The version number identifies a particular release of a particular module as it floats around the Internet.

Filename generation
> The archive of the distribution includes the version number of the primary module by default.

Upgrade indication
> Generally, numbers that increase numerically supersede previous versions. For this test, the number is considered a floating-point number, so 2.10 (which is really 2.1) is less than 2.9 (which must be the same as 2.90, by the same logic). To avoid confusion, if you've got two digits after the decimal point in one release, you shouldn't change it in the next without a very good reason.

Interface stability
> Generally, numbers that begin with 0 are alpha or beta, with external interfaces that may still be in flux. Also, most people use a major version number change (from 1.x to 2.x, etc.) to indicate a potential break in upward compatibility.

Recognition by the various CPAN tools
> The CPAN distribution management tools use the version number to track a particular release, and the CPAN installation tools can determine missing or out-of-date distributions.

Perl's own operators
> The use operator can be given a version number in addition to (or instead of) the import list, forcing the use operation to fail if the imported module is not equal or greater to that version:
> ```
> use Island::Plotting::Maps 1.10 qw{ map_debugger };
> ```

Generally, you can start with the 0.01 given by the template and increase it consistently with each new test release. Often, you can coordinate this version number with some source code control system.*

Now you're past the header information and down to the core of your module. In the template, it is indicated by a simple comment:

```
# Preloaded methods go here.
```

What? You didn't think the h2xs tool would even write the module for you, now did you? Anyway, this is where the code goes, usually as a series of subroutines, possibly preceded by some shared module data (using my declarations), and perhaps a few package variables (using our declarations in recent Perl versions). Following the code, you'll find your necessary true value:

```
1;
```

so the require (inside the use) doesn't abort.

Embedded Documentation

Immediately following the mandatory true value in the file, you'll find the __END__ marker:

```
__END__
```

This marker tells Perl that there's no Perl code anywhere later in the file and that the Perl parser can stop now.† Following the __END__ marker, you'll find the embedded documentation for the module:

```
# Below is stub documentation for your module. You'd better edit it!

=head1 NAME

Island::Plotting::Maps - Perl extension for blah blah blah

=head1 SYNOPSIS

  use Island::Plotting::Maps;
  blah blah blah

=head1 ABSTRACT

  This should be the abstract for Island::Plotting::Maps.
  The abstract is used when making PPD (Perl Package Description) files.
```

---

* The perlmod page includes an example that extracts the CVS/RCS version number for the module's version number.

† The data immediately following the __END__ marker is available by reading from the DATA filehandle, which is a great way to include a small amount of constant data with your program. However, that's not why we're doing that here.

```
    If you don't want an ABSTRACT you should also edit Makefile.PL to
    remove the ABSTRACT_FROM option.

=head1 DESCRIPTION

Stub documentation for Island::Plotting::Maps, created by h2xs. It looks like the
author of the extension was negligent enough to leave the stub
unedited.

Blah blah blah.

=head1 EXPORT

None by default.



=head1 SEE ALSO

Mention other useful documentation such as the documentation of
related modules or operating system documentation (such as man pages
in UNIX), or any relevant external documentation such as RFCs or
standards.

If you have a mailing list set up for your module, mention it here.

If you have a web site set up for your module, mention it here.

=head1 AUTHOR

Ginger Grant, <ginger@island.cocoanet>

=head1 COPYRIGHT AND LICENSE

Copyright 2002 by Ginger Grant

This library is free software; you can redistribute it and/or modify
it under the same terms as Perl itself.

=cut
```

This documentation is in POD format. The `perlpod` manpage describes the POD format in detail. Like Perl itself, POD is said to mean various things, such as Perl Online Documentation or Plain Old Documentation, and so on. To most of us, it's just POD.

As the template describes, you're expected to edit portions of this text to fit your particular module. In particular, leaving the `blah blah blah` is considered bad form.

The POD information is extracted automatically by the installation process to create the native documentation format, such as Unix manpages or HTML. Also, the `perldoc` command can locate POD in the installed scripts and modules and format it for the screen.

One nice thing about POD is that it can be interspersed with the Perl implementation code it describes. For example, from Chapter 12, you needed three subroutines for the Island::Plotting::Maps module. You can commingle the code and documentation. Each POD directive (a line beginning with an equal sign) switches from Perl mode (lines interpreted as Perl code) to POD mode (lines interpreted as documentation), and each line beginning with =cut switches back. Thus, the resulting file looks something like:

```
package Island::Plotting::Maps;
[... stuff down to the $VERSION setting above ...]

=head1 NAME

Island::Plotting::Maps - Plot maps on the island

=head1 SYNOPSIS

  use Island::Plotting::Maps;
  load_map("/usr/share/map/hawaii.map");
  scale_map(20, 20);
  draw_map(*STDOUT);

=head1 DESCRIPTION

This module draws maps.  [ more here ]

=over

=item load_map($filename)

This function [ more here ].

=cut

sub load_map {
  my $filename = shift;
  [ rest of subroutine ]
}

=item scale_map($x, $y)

This function [ more here ].

=cut

sub scale_map {
  my ($x, $y) = (shift, shift);
  [ rest of subroutine ]
}

=item draw_map($filehandle)
```

```
This function [ more here ].

=cut

sub draw_map {
  my $filehandle = shift;
  [ rest of subroutine ]
}

=back

=head1 SEE ALSO

"Map Reading for Dummies", "First Mates: why they're not the captain",
and be sure to consult with the Professor.

=head1 AUTHOR

Ginger Grant, <ginger@island.cocoanet>

=head1 COPYRIGHT AND LICENSE

Copyright 2002 by Ginger Grant

This library is free software; you can redistribute it and/or modify
it under the same terms as Perl itself.

=cut

1;
```

As you can see, the documentation for the subroutines is now very near the subroutine definition, in hope that as one gets updated, the other will be similarly changed. (Out-of-date documentation is often worse than no documentation at all because at least with no documentation at all, the user is forced to look at the source code.) Many modules in the CPAN do this. The penalty is a *very* slight increase in compile-time activity because the Perl parser has to skip over the embedded POD directives.

Whether you place your POD at the end of the file (as the template suggests) or intertwined with your code (as presented in the preceding paragraphs) the important thing to remember is always document your code. Even if it's just for you, a few months later, when your brain has been 42,000 other places before you look at the code again, you'll be glad to have those notes. Documentation is important.

Controlling the Distribution with Makefile.PL

The Perl developers have chosen to rely on the standard Unix make utility to build and install Perl itself, and that same mechanism is used for additional modules.* If you have a non-Unix system, a make-like utility should also be available. On Windows, for example, you may have dmake or another program. The command perl -V: make will tell you the name of your make utility program; if it says make='nmake', simply use nmake wherever you use make. In any case, you should call the controlling file a Makefile, even though its name may vary as well.

However, crafting a Makefile is tricky but repetitive. And what better way to accomplish a tricky but repetitive task than with a program? Since you're talking about Perl add-on modules, you know that Perl is available, so how about a Perl program to generate the Makefile?

That's exactly what happens. The distribution is required to contain a Makefile.PL, which is a Perl program to build a Makefile. Then from there, you use make (or something like it) to control all of the remaining tasks.

The h2xs tool generates a template Makefile.PL that you probably won't even need to touch for single-module distributions:

```
$ cat Makefile.PL
use 5.008;
use ExtUtils::MakeMaker;
# See lib/ExtUtils/MakeMaker.pm for details of how to influence
# the contents of the Makefile that is written.
WriteMakefile(
    'NAME'              => 'Island::Plotting::Maps',
    'VERSION_FROM'      => 'Maps.pm', # finds $VERSION
    'PREREQ_PM'              => { }, # e.g., Module::Name => 1.1
    ($] >= 5.005 ?     ## Add these new keywords supported since 5.005
      (ABSTRACT_FROM => 'Maps.pm', # retrieve abstract from module
       AUTHOR     => 'Ginger Grant <ginger@island.cocoanet>') : ()),
);
```

Yes, this is a Perl program. The WriteMakefile routine is defined by the ExtUtils::MakeMaker module (included with Perl) to generate a Makefile. As the developer of the module, use this makefile to build and test your module and prepare a distribution file:

```
$ perl Makefile.PL
Checking if your kit is complete...
Looks good
Writing Makefile for Island::Plotting::Maps
```

---

* The Module::Build module currently in development may replace all of that some day but is only in a prerelease form at the time of this writing.

The ultimate user of your distribution will execute the identical command at their site. However, the Makefile will most likely be different, reflecting the differences in installation locations, local policies, and even the C compiler and linking instructions appropriate for their architecture. It's a nice system that has worked quite well over the years.

The creation of the Makefile.PL (and resulting Makefile) is quite flexible. For example, you can run code to ask the person installing your module about the locations of other installed libraries or tools, or get options for variations in activity.*

The PREREQ_PM setting is important if your module depends on non-core Perl modules, especially if you plan to upload your code to the CPAN. Proper use of the prerequisites list can make installing your module nearly painless, and your user community will thank you.

Alternate Installation Locations (PREFIX=...)

Speaking of installation locations, the Makefile built by the default invocation of Makefile.PL presumes that the module will be installed in the system-wide Perl directory that all Perl programs can access directly with the built-in @INC path.

However, if you are testing a module, you certainly don't want to install it into the system directories, possibly corrupting a previous version of your module and breaking production programs.

Also, if you're not the system administrator, it's unlikely that you can change those central Perl directories because that would be a great way to insert a trojan horse for privileged users to stumble across.†

Luckily, the Makefile contains provisions for considering an alternate installation location for scripts, manpages, and libraries. The easiest way to specify an alternate location is with a PREFIX value as a parameter on the command line:

```
$ perl Makefile.PL PREFIX=~/Testing
Checking if your kit is complete...
Looks good
Writing Makefile for Island::Plotting::Maps
```

Although the messages don't indicate anything different, the Makefile will now install scripts to $PREFIX/bin, manpages below $PREFIX/man, and libraries below $PREFIX/lib/site_perl. In this case, you're selected a subdirectory of your home directory called Testing as the value of $PREFIX.

---

* Please keep the number of questions to a minimum, however. Most people are irritated when asked a series of questions, especially when they are just upgrading your module. If possible, store the answers in a configuration module that you install so that a later invocation of your installer can pull the previous answers as defaults.

† Even if you weren't the system administrator, you'd soon have all the powers of the system administrator.

If you were a project librarian, managing code for a team of developers, you might instead say something like:

```
$ perl Makefile.PL PREFIX=/path/to/shared/area
```

which then builds the files into a shared area. Of course, you'd need write privileges to such a directory, and the rest of the team would have to add the bin subdirectory to their PATH, the man subdirectory to their MANPATH, and the lib/site_perl directory to their @INC path, as you'll see shortly.

Trivial make test

Testing. Testing. Testing.

Testing is important. First, you should at least ensure that the code you've written even compiles before you install it and start playing with it. That test is free. You can invoke it directly from the newly created Makefile by simply typing make test, as in:

```
$ make test
cp Maps.pm blib/lib/Island/Plotting/Maps.pm
PERL_DL_NONLAZY=1 /usr/local/bin/perl "-MExtUtils::Command::MM" "-e" "test_harness(0,
'blib/lib', 'blib/arch')" t/*.t
t/1....ok
All tests successful.
Files=1, Tests=1,  1 wallclock secs ( 0.08 cusr +  0.04 csys =  0.12 CPU)
```

But what happened there?

First, the .pm file was copied to the testing staging area: the area headed by blib (build library) below the current directory.*

Next, the perl that invoked the Makefile.PL is called upon to run the *test harness*—a program that manages all test invocations and reports the results at the end.†

The test harness runs all files in the t subdirectory that end in .t in their natural order. You have only one file (created by h2xs), which looks like this:

```
$ cat t/1.t
# Before 'make install' is performed this script should be runnable with
# 'make test'. After 'make install' it should work as 'perl 1.t'

#########################

# change 'tests => 1' to 'tests => last_test_to_print';

use Test::More tests => 1;
```

---

* Had there been XS files or other more complex build steps, these also would have happened here.

† The perl that invoked the Makefile.PL is used for all configuration decisions. If you have more than one version of Perl installed on your system, be sure to execute the Makefile.PL with the correct one. From there, full paths are always used, so there's no chance of mixing anything else up.

```
BEGIN { use_ok('Island::Plotting::Maps') };

###########################

# Insert your test code below, the Test::More module is use()ed here so read
# its man page ( perldoc Test::More ) for help writing this test script.
```

It's a simple test program. The test pulls in the Test::More module, described further in Chapter 14. The import list for the module is treated specially; you're declaring that this test file consists of only one "test."

The test is given in the following line and attempts to use the module. If this succeeds, you get an "OK" sign, and the overall test file succeeds. This would fail with bad syntax, or perhaps if you forgot to have that true value at the end of the file.

In this example, the test succeeds, so you get a message for it and a summary of the CPU time used for the test.

Trivial make install

Since you know the module can at least compile, let's be daring and install it. Of course, you're installing it only into the path specified by the PREFIX in the earlier step, but that's enough to show how it would have worked for the ultimate user's installation.* The installation is triggered with make install:

```
$ make install
Manifying blib/man3/Island::Plotting::Maps.3
Installing /home/ginger/Testing/lib/site_perl/5.8.0/Island/Plotting/Maps.pm
Installing /home/ginger/Testing/man/man3/Island::Plotting::Maps.3
Writing /home/ginger/Testing/lib/site_perl/5.8.0/darwin/auto/Island/Plotting/Maps/.
packlist
Appending installation info to /home/ginger/Testing/lib/site_perl/5.8.0/darwin/
perllocal.pod
```

Note that you're installing the module below the $PREFIX/lib/site_lib directory (presuming a PREFIX of /home/ginger/Testing from earlier) and a manpage below $PREFIX/man (on Unix machines, in the Section 3 area for subroutines, for example). The manpage comes automatically when you extract the module's POD data and convert it to troff -man code, making it compatible with the Unix man command.†

---

* If you're playing along at home, be sure *not* to install this pretend module anywhere but a temporary, testing, directory. Although removing an installed module is generally difficult, you'll be able to simply delete the testing directory, along with its contents.

† On a non-Unix system, or even a few odd Unix systems, you'll see different behavior, but roughly the same overall result.

Trivial make dist

After some testing, you may decide it's time to share your work with friends and associates. To do this, make a single distribution file. Many mechanisms are available to do this, but the most common one on most modern Unix platforms is the GNU *gzip* compressed *tar* archive, commonly named with a .tar.gz or .tgz extension.

Again, with a simple make invocation (make dist), you end up with the required file:

```
$ make dist
rm -rf Island-Plotting-Maps-0.01
/usr/local/bin/perl "-MExtUtils::Manifest=manicopy,maniread" \
        -e "manicopy(maniread( ),'Island-Plotting-Maps-0.01', 'best');"
mkdir Island-Plotting-Maps-0.01
mkdir Island-Plotting-Maps-0.01/t
tar cvf Island-Plotting-Maps-0.01.tar Island-Plotting-Maps-0.01
Island-Plotting-Maps-0.01/
Island-Plotting-Maps-0.01/Changes
Island-Plotting-Maps-0.01/Makefile.PL
Island-Plotting-Maps-0.01/MANIFEST
Island-Plotting-Maps-0.01/Maps.pm
Island-Plotting-Maps-0.01/README
Island-Plotting-Maps-0.01/t/
Island-Plotting-Maps-0.01/t/1.t
rm -rf Island-Plotting-Maps-0.01
gzip --best Island-Plotting-Maps-0.01.tar
```

Now there's a file named Island-Plotting-Maps-0.01.tar.gz in the directory. The version number in the name comes from the module's $VERSION variable.*

Using the Alternate Library Location

The libraries are installed relative to the PREFIX specified earlier. If Ginger used a PREFIX of /home/ginger/Testing, you need to add the appropriate directory below it to the search path. The use lib directive of:

```
use lib "/home/ginger/Testing/lib/site_perl";
```

does the right thing to find the version-specific directory below it, as well as the architecture-specific directory below it, if needed (usually for architecture-specific files, such as compiled binaries).

You can also specify the include directory on the command line with a -M option:

```
$ perl -Mlib=/home/ginger/Testing/lib/site_perl myproggy
```

or a -I option:

```
$ perl -I /home/ginger/Testing/lib/site_perl myproggy
```

---

* If there's more than one module, you need to designate the primary module in the Makefile.PL.

or even by setting the PERL5LIB environment variable (using sh-like syntax here):

```
$ PERL5LIB=/home/ginger/Testing/lib/site_perl; export PERL5LIB
$ ./myproggy
```

However, the downside of any of these methods (other than the use lib method) is that they require you to do something more than just execute the file. If someone (or something) else (such as a coworker or a web server) executes your program, it's unlikely that the proper environment variable or command-line option will be present. Your program will fail because it can't find your locally installed module.

Use use lib, when you can. The other ways are useful mainly for trying out a new version of an old module before replacing the old module (and possibly breaking the programs that use it).

Exercise

The answers for all exercises can be found in the Appendix.

Exercise [30 min]

Package up the module from Chapter 12 as a distribution. Be sure to add the proper POD documentation for the subroutine. Test the module, install it locally, and then build a distribution file. If you have time, unpack the distribution into a different directory, pick a new prefix, and install it again to verify that the distribution archive contains everything necessary.

CHAPTER 14
Essential Testing

As briefly described in Chapter 13, a distribution contains a testing facility invoked from make test. This testing facility permits a module author to write and run tests during development and maintenance and the ultimate module installer to verify that the module works in the new environment.

Why have tests during development? One emerging school of thought states that the tests should be written first, even before the module is created, as a reflection of the module's specification. Of course, the initial test run against the unwritten module will show nearly complete failure. However, as functionality is added, proper functionality is verified immediately. (It's also handy to invoke the tests frequently as you code to make sure you're getting closer to the goal, not breaking more things.)

Certainly, errors may be found in the test suite. However, the defect rate for tests are usually far lower than the defect rate for complex module code; if a test fails, it's usually a good indication that there's more work to be done.

But even when Version 1.0 of the module is finally shipped, there's no need to abandon the test suite. Unless You code the mythical "bug-free module," there will be bug reports. Each bug report can (and should) be turned into a test.[*] While fixing the bug, the remaining tests prevent regression to a less functional version of the code—hence the name *regression testing*.

Then there's always the 1.1 or 2.0 releases to think about. When you want to add functionality, start by adding tests.[†] Because the existing tests ensure your upward compatibility, you can be confident that your new release does everything the old release did, and then some.

---

[*] If you're reporting a bug in someone else's code, you can generally assume that sending them a test for the bug will be appreciated. A patch would be appreciated even more!

[†] And writing the documentation at the same time, made easier by Test::Inline, as you'll see later.

Good tests also give small examples of what you meant in your documentation, in case your writing isn't clear.* Good tests also give confidence to the installer that this code is portable enough to work on both your system and his system, including all stated and unstated dependencies.

Testing is an art. Dozens of how-to-test books have been written and read, and often ignored. Mostly, it's important to remember everything you have ever done wrong while programming (or heard other people do), and then test that you didn't do it again for this project.

Test things that should break (throw exceptions or return false values) as well as things that should work. Test the edges. Test the middle. Test one more or one less than the edge. Test things one at a time. Test many things at once. If something should throw an exception, make sure it didn't also negatively affect the state of the world before it threw the exception. Pass extra parameters. Pass insufficient parameters. Mess up the capitalization on named parameters. Throw far too much data at it. Throw far too little. Test what happens for undef. And so on.

For example, suppose that you want to test Perl's sqrt function, which calculates square roots. It's obvious that you need to make sure it returns the right values when its parameter is 0, 1, 49, or 100. It's nearly as obvious to see that sqrt(0.25) should come out to be 0.5. You should also ensure that multiplying the value for sqrt(7) by itself gives something between 6.99999 and 7.00001.† You should make sure that sqrt(-1) yields a fatal error and that sqrt(-100) does too. See what happens when you request sqrt(&test_sub( )), and &test_sub returns a string of "10000". What does sqrt(undef) do? How about sqrt( ) or sqrt(1,1)? Maybe you want to give your function a googol: sqrt('1' . '0' x 100). Because this function is documented to work on $_ by default, you should ensure that it does so. Even a simple function such as sqrt should get a couple of dozen tests; if your code does more complex tasks than sqrt does, expect it to need more tests, too. There are never too many tests.

If you write the code and not just the tests, think about how to get every line of your code exercised at least once for full code coverage. (Are you testing the else clause? Are you testing every elsif case?) If you aren't writing the code or aren't sure, use the code coverage facilities.‡

Check out other test suites. The Perl distribution itself comes with thousands of tests, designed to verify that Perl compiles correctly on your machine in every possible way. Michael Schwern earned the title of "Perl Test Master" for getting the Perl

---

* Many modules we've used from the CPAN were documented more by test examples than by the actual POD. Of course, any really good example should be repeated in your module's POD documentation.

† Remember, floating-point numbers aren't always exact; there's usually a little roundoff. Feel free to write your tests to require more precision than this test implies but don't require more precision than you can get on another machine!

‡ Basic code coverage tools such as Devel::Cover are found in the CPAN.

core completely tested, and, still constantly beats the drum for "test! test! test!" in the community.

In summary, please write tests. Let's see how this is done.

What the Test Harness Does

Tests are usually invoked (either for the developer or the installer) using `make test`. The `Makefile` invokes the test harness, which eventually gets around to using the `Test::Harness` module to run the tests.

Each test lives in a separate `.t` file in the `t` directory at the top level of the distribution. Each test is invoked separately, so an `exit` or `die` terminates only that test file, not the whole testing process.

The test file communicates with the test harness through simple messages on standard output. The three most important messages are the test count, a success message, and a failure message.

An individual test file consists of one or more tests. These tests are numbered as small integers starting with one. The first thing a test file must announce to the test harness (on `STDOUT`) is the expected test number range, as a string `1..n`. For example, if there are 17 tests, the first line of output should be:

```
1..17
```

followed by a newline. The test harness uses the upper number here to verify that the test file hasn't just terminated early. If the test file is testing optional things and has no testing to do for this particular invocation, the string `1..0` suffices.

After the header, individual successes and failures are indicated by messages of the form `ok` *N* and `not ok` *N*. For example, here's a test of basic arithmetic. First, print the header:

```
print "1..4\n"; # the header
```

Now test that 1 plus 2 is 3:

```
if (1 + 2 == 3) {
  print "ok 1\n"; # first test is OK
} else {
  print "not ok 1\n"; # first test failed
}
```

You can also print the `not` if the test failed.[*] Don't forget the space!

```
print "not " unless 2 * 4 == 8;
print "ok 2\n";
```

---

[*] On some platforms, this may fail unnecessarily. For maximum portability, print the entire string of `ok` N or `not ok` N in one print step.

You could perhaps test that the results are close enough (important when dealing with floating-point values):

```
my $divide = 5 / 3;
print "not " if abs($divide - 1.666667) > 0.001; # too much error
print "ok 3\n";
```

Finally, you may want to deal with potential portability problems:

```
my $subtract = -3 + 3;
print +(($subtract eq "0" or $subtract eq "-0") ? "ok 4" : "not ok 4"), "\n";
```

As you can see, there are many styles for writing the tests. In ancient Perl development, you saw many examples of each style. Thanks to Michael Schwern and chromatic and the other Perl Testing Cabal members, you can now write these much more simply, using Test::Simple.

Writing Tests with Test::Simple

The Test::Simple module is included with the Perl distribution, starting in Perl 5.8.* Test::Simple automates the boring task of writing "ok 1", "ok 2", "ok 3", and so on, in your program. Test::Simple exports one subroutine, called (appropriately) ok. It's best illustrated by example. For the earlier code, you can rewrite it as:

```
use Test::Simple tests => 4;

ok(1 + 2 == 3, '1 + 2 == 3');
ok(2 * 4 == 8, '2 * 4 == 8');
my $divide = 5 / 3;
ok(abs($divide - 1.666667) < 0.001, '5 / 3 == (approx) 1.666667');
my $subtract = -3 + 3;
ok(($subtract eq "0" or $subtract eq "-0"), '-3 + 3 == 0');
```

Ahh. So much simpler. The use not only pulls the module in but also defines the number of tests. This generates the 1..4 header. Each ok test evaluates its first argument. If the argument is true, it prints the proper ok message. If not, it prints the proper not ok message. For this particular example, the output looks like:†

```
1..4
ok 1 - 1 + 2 == 3
ok 2 - 2 * 4 == 8
ok 3 - 5 / 3 == (approx) 1.666667
ok 4 - -3 + 3 == 0
```

The ok N messages are followed with the labels given as the second parameters. This is great for identifying each test, especially because the numbers 1 through 4 don't

---

* Older Perl versions back to 5.004_03 can install the same module from the CPAN.

† Don't be misled when reading the mathematics of the output. The first number and the dash on each ok line are just labels; Perl isn't telling you that 1 - 1 + 2 == 3!

appear in the original test anymore. The test harness ignores this information, unless you invoke make test with make test TEST_VERBOSE=1, in which case, the information is displayed for each test.

What if a test fails? If you change the first test to 1 + 2 = = 4, you get:

```
1..4
not ok 1 - 1 + 2 == 4
#     Failed test (1.t at line 4)
ok 2 - 2 * 4 == 8
ok 3 - 5 / 3 == (approx) 1.666667
ok 4 - -3 + 3 == 0
# Looks like you failed 1 tests of 4.
```

The ok 1 became not ok 1. But also notice the extra message indicating the failed test, including its file and line number. Messages preceded by a pound-sign comment marker are merely comments, and are (mostly) ignored by the test harness.

For many people, Test::Simple is simple enough to use for a wide range of tests. However, as your Perl hackery evolves, you'll want to step up to the next level of Perl testing hackery as well, with Test::More.

Writing Tests with Test::More

Like Test::Simple, Test::More is included with the distribution starting with Perl 5.8. The Test::More module is upward-compatible with Test::Simple, so you can simply change the module name to start using it. In this example so far, you can use:

```
use Test::More tests => 4;

ok(1 + 2 == 3, '1 + 2 == 3');
ok(2 * 4 == 8, '2 * 4 == 8');
my $divide = 5 / 3;
ok(abs($divide - 1.666667) < 0.001, '5 / 3 == (approx) 1.666667');
my $subtract = -3 + 3;
ok(($subtract eq "0" or $subtract eq "-0"), '-3 + 3 == 0');
```

You get nearly the same output you got with Test::Simple, but there's that nasty little 4 constant in the first line. That's fine once shipping the code, but if you're testing, retesting, and adding more tests, it can be a bit painful to keep the number in sync with the data. You can change that to no_plan,[*] as in:

```
use Test::More "no_plan";        # during development

ok(1 + 2 == 3, '1 + 2 == 3');
ok(2 * 4 == 8, '2 * 4 == 8');
my $divide = 5 / 3;
ok(abs($divide - 1.666667) < 0.001, '5 / 3 == (approx) 1.666667');
```

---

[*] You can do this with Test::Simple as well.

```
my $subtract = -3 + 3;
ok(($subtract eq "0" or $subtract eq "-0"), '-3 + 3 == 0');
```

The output is now rearranged:

```
ok 1 - 1 + 2 == 3
ok 2 - 2 * 4 == 8
ok 3 - 5 / 3 == (approx) 1.666667
ok 4 - -3 + 3 == 0
1..4
```

Note that the number of tests are now at the end. The test harness knows that if it doesn't see a header, it's expecting a footer. If the number of tests disagree or there's no footer (and no header), it's a broken result. You can use this while developing, but be sure to put the final number of tests in the script before you ship it as real code.

But wait: there's more (to Test::More). Instead of a simple yes/no, you can ask if two values are the same:

```
use Test::More "no_plan";

is(1 + 2, 3, '1 + 2 is 3');
is(2 * 4, 8, '2 * 4 is 8');
```

Note that you've gotten rid of numeric equality and instead asked if "this is that." On a successful test, this doesn't give much advantage, but on a failed test, you get much more interesting output. The result of this:

```
use Test::More "no_plan";

is(1 + 2, 3, '1 + 2 is 3');
is(2 * 4, 6, '2 * 4 is 6');
```

is the interesting:

```
ok 1 - 1 + 2 is 3
not ok 2 - 2 * 4 is 6
#     Failed test (1.t at line 4)
#          got: '8'
#     expected: '6'
1..2
# Looks like you failed 1 tests of 2.
```

Of course, this is an error in the test, but note that the output told you what happened: you got an 8 but were expecting a 6.* This is far better than just "something went wrong" as before. There's also a corresponding isnt( ) when you want to compare for inequality rather than equality.

---

* More precisely: you got an '8' but were expecting a '6'. Did you notice that these are strings? The is test checks for string equality. If you don't want that, just build an ok test instead. Or try cmp_ok, coming up in a moment.

What about that third test, where the value had to be less than a tolerance? Well, just use the `cmp_ok` routine instead:

```
use Test::More "no_plan";

my $divide = 5 / 3;
cmp_ok(abs($divide - 1.666667), '<' , 0.001,
    '5 / 3 should be (approx) 1.666667');
```

If the test given in the second argument fails between the first and third arguments, then you get a descriptive error message with both of the values and the comparison, rather than a simple pass/fail value as before.

How about that last test? You wanted to see if the result was a 0 or minus 0 (on the rare systems that give back a minus 0). You can do that with the `like` function:

```
use Test::More "no_plan";

my $subtract = -3 + 3;
like($subtract, qr/^-?0$/, '-3 + 3 == 0');
```

Here, you'll take the string form of the first argument and attempt to match it against the second argument. The second argument is typically a regular expression object (created here with `qr`) but can also be a simple string, which is converted to a regular expression object. The string form can even be written as if it was (almost) a regular expression:

```
like($subtract, q/^-?0$/, '-3 + 3 == 0');
```

The advantage to using the string form is that it is portable back to older Perls.*

If the match succeeds, it's a good test. If not, the original string and the regex are reported along with the test failure. You can change `like` to `unlike` if you expect the match to fail instead.

For object-oriented modules, you might want to ensure that object creation has succeeded. For this, `isa_ok` and `can_ok` give good interface tests:

```
use Test::More "no_plan";

use Horse;
my $trigger = Horse->named("Trigger");
isa_ok($trigger, "Horse");
isa_ok($trigger, "Animal");
can_ok($trigger, $_) for qw(eat color);
```

This results in:

```
ok 1 - The object isa Horse
ok 2 - The object isa Animal
ok 3 - Horse->can('eat')
```

---

* The qr// form wasn't introduced until Perl 5.005.

```
ok 4 - Horse->can('color')
1..4
```

Here you're testing that it's a horse, but also that it's an animal, and that it can both eat and return a color.* You could further test to ensure that each horse has a unique name:

```
use Test::More "no_plan";

use Horse;

my $trigger = Horse->named("Trigger");
isa_ok($trigger, "Horse");

my $tv_horse = Horse->named("Mr. Ed");
isa_ok($tv_horse, "Horse");

# Did making a second horse affect the name of the first horse?
is($trigger->name, "Trigger", "Trigger's name is correct");
is($tv_horse->name, "Mr. Ed", "Mr. Ed's name is correct");
is(Horse->name, "a generic Horse");
```

The output of this is:

```
ok 1 - The object isa Horse
ok 2 - The object isa Horse
ok 3 - Trigger's name is correct
ok 4 - Mr. Ed's name is correct
not ok 5
#     Failed test (1.t at line 13)
#          got: 'an unnamed Horse'
#     expected: 'a generic Horse'
1..5
# Looks like you failed 1 tests of 5.
```

Oops! Look at that. You wrote a generic Horse, but the string really is an unnamed Horse. That's an error in the test, not in the module, so you should correct that test error and retry. Unless, of course, the module's spec actually called for 'a generic Horse'.

Again, don't be afraid to just write the tests and test the module. If you get either one wrong, the other will generally catch it.

Even the use can be tested by Test::More:

```
use Test::More "no_plan";

BEGIN { use_ok("Horse") }

my $trigger = Horse->named("Trigger");
```

---

* Well, you're testing to see that it can('eat') and can('color'). You haven't checked whether it really can use those method calls to do what you want!

```
isa_ok($trigger, "Horse");
# .. other tests as before ..
```

The difference between doing this as a test and doing it as a simple use is that the test won't completely abort if the use fails, although many other tests are likely to fail as well. It's also counted as one of the tests, so you get a "test succeeded" for free even if all it does is compile properly to help pad your success numbers for the weekly status report.

The use is placed inside a BEGIN block so any exported subroutines are properly declared for the rest of the program, as recommended by the documentation. For most object-oriented modules, this won't matter because they don't export subroutines.

Conditional Tests

If you write tests directly from the specification before you've written the code, the tests are expected to fail. You can include some of your tests inside a TODO block to include them for test count but denote them as unavailable at the same time. For example, suppose you haven't taught your horses how to talk yet:

```
use Test::More 'no_plan';

use_ok("Horse");
my $tv_horse = Horse->named("Mr. Ed");
TODO: {
  local $TODO = "haven't taught Horses to talk yet";

  can_ok($tv_horse, "talk");  # he can talk!
}
is($tv_horse->name, "Mr. Ed", "I am Mr. Ed!");
```

Here, the test is inside a TODO block, setting a package $TODO variable with the reason why the items are unfinished:*

```
ok 1 - use Horse;
not ok 2 - Horse->can('talk') # TODO haven't taught Horses to talk yet
#     Failed (TODO) test (1.t at line 7)
#     Horse->can('talk') failed
ok 3 - I am Mr. Ed!
1..3
```

Note that the TODO test counts toward the total number of tests. Also note that the message about why the test is a TODO test is displayed as a comment. The comment has a special form, noted by the test harness, so you will see it during a make test run.

---

* TODO tests require Test::Harness Version 2.0 or later, which comes with Perl 5.8, but in earlier releases, they have to be installed from the CPAN .

You can have multiple TODO tests in a given block, but only one reason per block, so it's best to group things that are related but use different blocks for different reasons.

More Complex Tests (Multiple Test Scripts)

Initially, the h2xs program gives you a single testing file, t/1.t.[*] You can stick all your tests into this file, but it generally makes more sense to break the tests into logical groups.

The easiest way to add additional tests is to create t/2.t. That's it—just bump the 1 to a 2. You don't need to change anything in the Makefile.PL or in the test harness: the file is noticed and executed automatically.

You can keep adding files until you get to 9.t, but once you add 10.t, you might notice that it gets executed between 1.t and 2.t. Why? Because the tests are always executed in sorted order. This is a good thing because it lets you ensure that the most fundamental tests are executed before the more exotic tests, simply by controlling the names.

Many people choose to rename the files to reflect a specific ordering and purpose by using names like 01-core.t, 02-basic.t, 03-advanced.t, 04-saving.t, and so on. The first two digits control the testing order, while the rest of the name gives a hint about the general area of testing. Whatever plan you decide to use, stick with it, document it if necessary, and remember that the default order is controlled by the name.

Testing Things That Write to STDOUT and STDERR

One advantage to using the ok( ) functions (and friends) is that they don't write to STDOUT directly, but to a filehandle secretly duplicated from STDOUT when your test script begins. If you don't change STDOUT in your program, of course, this is a moot point. But let's say you wanted to write test a routine that writes something to STDOUT, such as making sure a horse eats properly:

```
use Test::More 'no_plan';
use_ok 'Horse';
isa_ok(my $trigger = Horse->named('Trigger'), 'Horse');

open STDOUT, ">test.out" or die;
$trigger->eat("hay");
close STDOUT;
```

---

[*] As of Perl 5.8, that is. Earlier versions create a test.pl file, which is still run from a test harness during make test, but the output wasn't captured in the same way.

```
open T, "test.out" or die;
my @contents = <T>;
close T;
is(join("", @contents), "Trigger eats hay.\n", "Trigger ate properly");

END { unlink "test.out" }  # clean up after the horses
```

Note that just before you start testing the eat method, you (re-)open STDOUT to your temporary output file. The output from this method ends up in the test.out file. Bring the contents of that file in and give it to the is( ) function. Even though you've closed STDOUT, the is( ) function can still access the original STDOUT, and thus the test harness sees the proper ok or not ok messages.

If you create temporary files like this, please note that your current directory is the same as the test script (even if you're running make test from the parent directory). Also pick fairly safe cross-platform names if you want people to be able to use and test your module portably.

Exercise

The answers for all exercises can be found in the Appendix.

Exercise [60 min]

Write a module distribution, starting from the tests first.

Your goal is to create a module My::List::Util that exports two routines on request: sum and shuffle. The sum routine takes a list of values and returns the numeric sum. The shuffle routine takes a list of values and randomly shuffles the ordering, returning the list.

Start with sum. Write the tests, and then add the code. You'll know you're done when the tests pass. Now include tests for shuffle, and then add the implementation for shuffle.

Be sure to update the documentation and MANIFEST file as you go along.

If you can pair up with someone on this exercise, even better. One of you writes the test for sum and the implementation code for shuffle, and the other does the opposite. Swap the t/* files, and see if you can locate any errors!

## CHAPTER 15

Contributing to CPAN

Besides allowing others in your organization receive the benefits of these wonderful modules and distributions you've created, you may wish to contribute to the Perl community at large. The mechanism for sharing your work is called the Comprehensive Perl Archive Network, or CPAN for short.

The Comprehensive Perl Archive Network

The CPAN is the result of many volunteers working together, many of whom were originally operating their own little (or big) Perl FTP sites back before that Web thing came along. They got coordinated on their *perl-packrats* mailing list in late 1993 and decided that disk was getting cheap enough that the same information should be replicated on all sites, rather than having specialization on each site. The idea took about a year to ferment, and Jarkko Hietaniemi established his Finnish FTP site as the CPAN mothership, from which all other mirrors could draw their daily or hourly updates.

Part of the work involved rearranging and organizing the separate archives. Places were established for Perl binaries for non-Unix architectures, scripts, and Perl's source code itself. But the modules portion has come to be the largest and most interesting part of the CPAN.

The modules in the CPAN are organized as a symbolic-link tree in hierarchical functional categories, pointing to author directories where the actual files are located. The modules area also contains indicies that are generally in easy-to-parse-with-Perl formats, such as the `Data::Dumper` output for the detailed module index. Of course, these indicies are all derived automatically from databases at the master server using Perl programs. (Often, the mirroring of the CPAN from one server to another is done with a now-ancient Perl program called `mirror.pl`.)

From its small start of a few mirror machines, the CPAN has now grown to over 200 public archives in all corners of the Net, all churning away updating at least daily, sometimes as frequently as hourly. No matter where you are in the world, you can find a nearby CPAN mirror from which to pull the latest goodies.

Getting Prepared

To contribute to the CPAN, you need two things:

- Something to contribute, hopefully already in the shape of a module
- A Perl Authors Upload Server (PAUSE) ID

The PAUSE ID is your ticket to contributing to the CPAN. You get a PAUSE ID just for the asking. The details are described at *http://www.cpan.org/modules/04pause.html*. You need to fill out a web form (linked from there) with a few basic details such as your name, home web page, email address, and your preferred PAUSE ID. At the moment, PAUSE IDs must be between four and nine characters. (Some legacy PAUSE IDs are only three characters long.)*

Once you have your PAUSE ID, you need to think globally about your contribution. Because your module will probably be used in programs along with other modules from other authors, you need to ensure that the package names for modules don't collide or confuse. Consult with the module-naming volunteers listening at the *modules@perl.org* mailing list to get a name or hierarchy of names for your module or related modules.

Before you send your first email to the module czars, it's probably a good idea to do a few things first:

- Look at the current module list. Get an idea for how things are named. Better yet, are you just reinventing a subset of something that already exists, or can you simply contribute your work as a patch to another module?
- Visit the list archives (pointers can be found at *http://lists.perl.org*) to see what the typical conversations look like. That might help you to avoid shock at your response, or better phrase your initial request.
- Above all, get it in your head that this whole process is run by volunteers who aren't perfect and are doing this in their spare time for the good of the Perl community. Have patience. Have tolerance.

Preparing Your Distribution

Once you've gotten your module name settled and you've tested your module with its new name (if needed), you should make sure your distribution is ready for prime

---

* Originally, the PAUSE IDs had to be five characters or less, until Randal wanted his MERLYN ID, and the appropriate accommodation was made.

time. While this is similar to releasing a distribution inhouse, as described in Chapter 14, you might want to ensure a few additional things about your distribution:

- Create a README file. This file is automatically extracted to a separate file on the CPAN archives and lets someone view or download just the key facts about your distribution before fetching or unpacking the rest.

- Make and test your Makefile.PL. Modules without a Makefile.PL are accepted via PAUSE to go into the CPAN but usually get a grimace from those of us who download your stuff because we might have to figure out how to build and install your distribution.

- Bring your MANIFEST up to date. If you add files that should be part of the distribution, they also need to be in the MANIFEST. One quick trick is to clean things up as you would want them in the distribution, and then invoke make manifest, which updates the MANIFEST file to be exactly what you are holding at the moment.

- Have a logical distribution version number. The Makefile.PL file should specify either a VERSION value or a VERSION_FROM value. If you have a single module (such as a .pm file) in your distribution, it's usually best to grab the version number from there with VERSION_FROM. If you have multiple files, either designate one of them as the one you'll always update just before a new release or use the VERSION within the Makefile.PL instead. Also keep in mind that your version number must always increase numerically for newer versions of your distribution.

- Have tests! Reread Chapter 14 if you must. There's nothing that builds more confidence in an installed distribution than at least a few dozen tests that are run during the installation phase.

- Invoke make disttest, which builds a distribution archive of everything in MANIFEST, unpacks the archive into a separate directory, and then runs the tests on your distribution. If that doesn't work for you, you can't expect it to work for anyone else who downloads your distribution from the CPAN.

Uploading Your Distribution

Once you have your distribution ready to share, visit the PAUSE web page at *http://pause.perl.org/* and log in using your PAUSE ID and PAUSE password. The menu has many things you can do; there are two processes to complete for your distribution:

- Upload the distribution archive
- Edit the module metadata

First is the upload, which you can do using an HTTP upload, a web fetch, or an FTP transfer. The HTTP upload is convenient if the distribution archive is on the same computer as your web browser. Otherwise, if you can move the file into a place where it can be fetched (even a private URL will do), you can use the web fetch. If neither option works, then FTP the file to PAUSE FTP server.

After the file is uploaded, you should edit the metadata. Again, select the appropriate menu item from the PAUSE page and follow the instructions. The metadata helps others decide if you're just releasing an alpha version instead of a final release, and whether or not the module needs additional support, like a C compiler.

Within a short period of time, your upload will appear in the mothership CPAN archive, and then over the following day, will propagate around the world, just waiting for its first download.

Announcing the Module

Of course, nobody will know that your module exists until they notice it. Your module gets noticed automatically in many places, such as:

- The "Recent modules" page of *http://search.cpan.org*
- The "new modules" section of *http://use.perl.org*
- A daily announcement in the "perl news" mailing list
- An IRC 'bot on a few of the Perl-related IRC channels announces uploads as soon as they become available
- An update or an uninstalled module in the CPAN shell, CPAN.pm

For greater visibility, you can also prepare a short notice to be posted to the Usenet *comp.lang.perl.announce* newsgroup. Just post the notice, and within a day or two, your news posting will be whisking around to news servers all over the globe.

Testing on Multiple Platforms

Many volunteers have organized a *smoke test* of your module on many platforms. Simply as a result of uploading your registered module to the CPAN, your module will be downloaded and make test'ed on many different kinds of machines. You can view the results of the tests at *http://testers.cpan.org*. You should note any failures and consider using the feedback to release a new distribution that works more portably.

Consider Writing an Article or Giving a Talk

Many of the short talks at Perl conferences involve the author of a distribution talking about their own work. After all, who is better qualified to help others use your module than you?

If the idea of proposing a conference talk intimidates you a bit, or you don't want to wait that long, look to your local Perl user group. They're generally looking for speakers (usually for the meeting coming up in the next week or two), and the group size is usually small enough to be a nice casual setting. You can generally find a Perl user group near you by looking on the Perl Mongers web site at *http://www.pm.org*. If you can't find one, start one!

Exercise

The answers for all exercises can be found in the Appendix.

Exercise

Write a module to solve the halting problem. Release the code to the CPAN. Be sure to include the tests. (Hint: how long will the tests take to run on modern hardware?)

APPENDIX

Answers to Exercises

This appendix contains the answers to the exercises presented throughout the book.

Answers for Chapter 2

Exercise 1

Here's one way to do it. First, start with the package directive and use strict:

```
package Oogaboogoo::date;
use strict;
```

Then define the constant arrays to hold the mappings for day-of-week and month names:

```
my @day = qw(ark dip wap sen pop sep kir);
my @mon = qw(diz pod bod rod sip wax lin sen kun fiz nap dep);
```

Next, define the subroutine for day-of-week-number to name. Note that this subroutine will be accessible as Oogaboogoo::date::day:

```
sub day {
  my $num = shift @_;
  die "$num is not a valid day number"
    unless $num >= 0 and $num <= 6;
  $day[$num];
}
```

Similarly, you have the subroutine for the month-of-year-number to name:

```
sub mon {
  my $num = shift @_;
  die "$num is not a valid month number"
    unless $num >= 0 and $num <= 11;
  $mon[$num];
}
```

Finally, the mandatory true value at the end of the package:

```
1;
```

Name this file date.pl within a directory of Oogaboogoo in one of the directories given in your @INC variable, such as the current directory.

Exercise 2

Here's one way to do it. Pull in the .pl file from a place in your @INC path:

```
use strict;
require 'Oogaboogoo/date.pl';
```

Then get the information for the current time:

```
my($sec, $min, $hour, $mday, $mon, $year, $wday) = localtime;
```

Then use the newly defined subroutines for the conversions:

```
my $day_name = Oogaboogoo::date::day($wday);
my $mon_name = Oogaboogoo::date::mon($mon);
```

The year number is offset by 1900 for historical purposes, so you need to fix that:

```
$year += 1900;
```

Finally, it's time for the output:

```
print "Today is $day_name, $mon_name $mday, $year.\n";
```

Answers for Chapter 3

Exercise 1

They're all referring to the same thing, except for the second one, ${$ginger[2]}[1]. That one is the same as $ginger[2][1], whose base is the array @ginger, rather than the scalar $ginger.

Exercise 2

First, construct the hash structure:

```
my @gilligan = qw(red_shirt hat lucky_socks water_bottle);
my @professor = qw(sunscreen water_bottle slide_rule batteries radio);
my @skipper = qw(blue_shirt hat jacket preserver sunscreen);
my %all = (
  "Gilligan" => \@gilligan,
  "Skipper" => \@skipper,
  "Professor" => \@professor,
);
```

Then pass it to the first subroutine:

```
check_items_for_all(\%all);
```

In the subroutine, the first parameter is a hashref, so dereference it to get the keys and the corresponding values:

```
sub check_items_for_all {
  my $all = shift;
  for my $person (sort keys %$all) {
    check_required_items($person, $all->{$person});
  }
}
```

From there, call the original subroutine:

```
sub check_required_items {
  my $who = shift;
  my $items = shift;
  my @required = qw(preserver sunscreen water_bottle jacket);
  my @missing = ( );
  for my $item (@required) {
    unless (grep $item eq $_, @$items) { # not found in list?
      print "$who is missing $item.\n";
      push @missing, $item;
    }
  }
  if (@missing) {
    print "Adding @missing to @$items for $who.\n";
    push @$items, @missing;
  }
}
```

Answers for Chapter 4

Exercise 1

The curly braces of the anonymous hash constructor make a reference to a hash. That's a scalar (as are all references), so it's not suitable to use alone as the value of a hash. Perhaps this code's author intended to assign to scalar variables (like $passenger_1 and $passenger_2) instead of to hashes. But you can fix the problem simply by changing the two pairs of curly braces to parentheses.

If you tried running this, Perl may have given you a helpful diagnostic message as a warning. If you didn't get the warning, perhaps you didn't have warnings turned on, either with the -w switch or with the use warnings pragma. Even if you don't usually use Perl's warnings, you should enable them during debugging. (How long would it take you to debug this without Perl's warnings to help you? How long would it take to enable Perl's warnings? 'Nuff said.)

What if you got the warning message but couldn't tell what it meant? That's what the perldiag manpage is for. Warning texts need to be concise because they're compiled into the perl binary (the program that runs your Perl code). But perldiag should list all the messages you should ever get from Perl, along with a longer explanation of what each one means, why it's a problem, and how to fix it.

If you want to be ultimately lazy, you can add use diagnostics; at the beginning of your program, and any error message will look itself up in the documentation and display the entire detailed message. Don't leave this in production code, however, unless you like burning a lot of CPU cycles every time your program starts, whether or not an error occurs.

Exercise 2

You will be keeping count of how much data has been sent to all machines, so at the start, set the variable $all to a name that will stand in for all of them. It should be a name that will never be used for any real machine, of course. Storing it in a variable is convenient for writing the program and makes it easy to change later.

```
my $all = "**all machines**";
```

The input loop is nearly the same as given in the chapter, but it skips comment lines. Also, it keeps a second running total, filed under $all.

```
my %total_bytes;
while (<>) {
  next if /^#/;
  my ($source, $destination, $bytes) = split;
  $total_bytes{$source}{$destination} += $bytes;
  $total_bytes{$source}{$all} += $bytes;
}
```

Next, make a sorted list. This holds the names of the source machines in descending order of total transferred bytes. This list is used for the outer for loop. (Rather than using a temporary array, @sources, you might have put the sort directly into the parens of the for loop.)

```
my @sources =
  sort { $total_bytes{$b}{$all} <=> $total_bytes{$a}{$all} }
  keys %total_bytes;

for my $source (@sources) {
  my @destinations =
    sort { $total_bytes{$source}{$b} <=> $total_bytes{$source}{$a} }
    keys %{ $total_bytes{$source} };
  print "$source: $total_bytes{$source}{$all} total bytes sent\n";
  for my $destination (@destinations) {
    next if $destination eq $all;
    print "  $source => $destination:",
      " $total_bytes{$source}{$destination} bytes\n";
  }
}
```

```
    print "\n";
  }
```

Inside the loop, print out the total number of bytes sent from that source machine, then make sorted list of the destination files (similar to the list in @sources). As you step through that list, use next to skip over the dummy $all item. Because that item will be at the head of the sorted list, why wasn't shift used to discard it, since that would avoid checking repeatedly for $all inside the inner loop? The answer is in this footnote.*

You can simplify this program, perhaps. The subexpression $total_bytes{$source} is used many times in the large output for loop (and twice in the input loop as well). That can be replaced by a simple scalar, initialized at the top of the loop:

```
for my $source (@sources) {
  my $tb = $total_bytes{$source};
  my @destinations = sort { $tb{$b} <=> $tb{$a} } keys %$tb;
  print "$source: $tb{$all} total bytes sent\n";
  for my $destination (@destinations) {
    next if $destination eq $all;
    print "  $source => $destination: $tb{$destination} bytes\n";
  }
  print "\n";
}
```

This makes the code shorter and (likely) a bit faster as well. Give yourself extra credit if you thought to do this. Also give yourself extra credit if you thought that it might be too confusing and decided not to make the change.

Answers for Chapter 5

Exercise 1

```
use Storable;

my $all = "**all machines**";
my $data_file = "total_bytes.data";

my %total_bytes;
if (-e $data_file) {
  my $data = retrieve $data_file;
  %total_bytes = %$data;
}

while (<>) {
```

---

* Even though the dummy item will sort to the head of the sorted list, it won't necessarily be the first item in the list. If a machine sent data to just one other, that destination machine's total will be equal to the source machine's total output, so that list could sort in either order.

```
      next if /^#/;
      my ($source, $destination, $bytes) = split;
      $total_bytes{$source}{$destination} += $bytes;
      $total_bytes{$source}{$all} += $bytes;
  }

  store \%total_bytes, $data_file;

  ### remainder of program is unchanged
```

This is similar to what you saw in Chapter 4, but now it uses Storable.

Near the top, put the filename into a variable. You can then retrieve the data but only if the data file already exists.

After reading the data, use Storable again to write it back out to the same disk file.

If you chose to write the hash's data to a file the hard way, by writing your own code and your own file format, you're working too hard. More to the point, unless you're extraordinarily talented or spend way too long on this exercise, you almost certainly have bugs in your serialization routines, or at least flaws in your file format.

Exercise 2

There should probably be some checks to ensure that Storable was successful. It will catch some errors (and die), but it will simply return undef for some. See the documentation for Storable. (Of course, if you checked the return values from store and retrieve, you should give yourself extra credit on the previous exercise.)

The program should save the old data file (if any) under a backup filename so that it's easy to revert the latest additions. In fact, it could even keep several backups, such as the last week's worth.

It might also be nice to be able to print the output without having any new input data. As it's written, this can be done by giving an empty file (such as /dev/null) as the input. However there should be an easier way. The output functionality could be separated entirely from the updating, in fact.

Answer for Chapter 6

Exercise

```
  sub gather_mtime_between {
    my($begin, $end) = @_;
    my @files;
    my $gatherer = sub {
      my $timestamp = (stat $_)[9];
      unless (defined $timestamp) {
```

```
        warn "Can't stat $File::Find::name: $!, skipping\n";
        return;
      }
    push @files, $File::Find::name if
      $timestamp >= $begin and $timestamp <= $end;
  };
  my $fetcher = sub { @files };
  ($gatherer, $fetcher);
}
```

This code is pretty straightforward. The main challenge is getting the item names correct. When using stat inside the callback, the filename is $_, but when returning the filename (or reporting it to the user), the name is $File::Find::name.

If the stat fails for some reason, the timestamp will be undef. (That can happen, for example, if it finds a dangling symbolic link.) In that case, the callback simply warns the user and returns early. If you omit that check, you can get warnings of an undefined value during the comparison with $begin and $end.

When you run the completed program with this subroutine, your output should show only file modification dates on the previous Monday (unless you changed the code to use a different day of the week, of course).

Answers for Chapter 7

Exercise 1

```
my @sorted =
  map $_->[0],
  sort { $a->[1] <=> $b->[1] }
  map [$_, -s $_],
  glob "/bin/*";
```

Using the -s operator to determine the file's size is an expensive operation; by caching its value you can save some time. How much? Let's see in the next exercise's answer.

Exercise 2

```
use Benchmark qw(timethese);

timethese( -2, {
  Ordinary => q{
    my @results = sort { -s $a <=> -s $b } glob "/bin/*";
  },
  Schwartzian => q{
    my @sorted =
      map $_->[0],
      sort { $a->[1] <=> $b->[1] }
      map [$_, -s $_],
```

```
      glob "/bin/*";
    },
  });
```

On the 33-element /bin on my laptop, I (Randal) was seeing 260 iterations per second of the Ordinary implementation and roughly 500 per second of the Schwartzian implementation, so writing the complex code saved about half of the execution time. On a 74-element /etc, the Schwartzian Transform was nearly three times as fast. In general, the more items sorted, the more expensive the computed function, and the better you can expect the Schwartzian Transform to perform. That doesn't even count the burden on the monkey—er, I mean the operating system.

Exercise 3

```
my @dictionary_sorted =
  map $_->[0],
  sort { $a->[1] cmp $b->[1] }
  map {
    my $string = $_;
    $string =~ tr/A-Z/a-z/;
    $string =~ tr/a-z//cd;
    [ $_, $string ];
  } @input_list;
```

Inside the second map, which executes first, make a copy of $_. (If you don't, you'll mangle the data.)

Exercise 4

```
sub data_for_path {
  my $path = shift;
  if (-f $path or -l $path) {
    return undef;
  }
  if (-d $path) {
    my %directory;
    opendir PATH, $path or die "Cannot opendir $path: $!";
    my @names = readdir PATH;
    closedir PATH;
    for my $name (@names) {
      next if $name eq "." or $name eq "..";
      $directory{$name} = data_for_path("$path/$name");
    }
    return \%directory;
  }
  warn "$path is neither a file nor a directory\n";
  return undef;
}

sub dump_data_for_path {
  my $path = shift;
```

```
  my $data = shift;
  my $prefix = shift || "";
  print "$prefix$path";
  if (not defined $data) { # plain file
    print "\n";
    return;
  }
  my %directory = %$data;
  if (%directory) {
    print ", with contents of:\n";
    for (sort keys %directory) {
      dump_data_for_path($_, $directory{$_}, "$prefix  ");
    }
  } else {
    print ", an empty directory\n";
  }
}
dump_data_for_path(".", data_for_path("."));
```

By adding a third (prefix) parameter to the dumping subroutine, you can ask it to indent its output. By default, the prefix is empty, of course.

When the subroutine calls itself, it adds two spaces to the end of the prefix. Why the end and not the beginning? Because it's comprised of spaces, either end will work. By using trailing spaces, you can call the subroutine like this:

```
dump_data_for_path(".", data_for_path("."), "> ");
```

This invocation quotes the entire output by prefixing each line with the given string. You can (in some hypothetical future version of this program) use such quoting to denote NFS-mounted directories, or other special items.

Answers for Chapter 8

Exercise 1

Here's one way to do it. First define the Animal class, with a single method:

```
use strict;
{ package Animal;
  sub speak {
    my $class = shift;
    print "a $class goes ", $class->sound, "!\n";
  }
}
```

Now define each subclass with a specific sound:

```
{ package Cow;
  our @ISA = qw(Animal);
  sub sound { "moooo" }
}
{ package Horse;
```

```
    our @ISA = qw(Animal);
    sub sound { "neigh" }
  }
  { package Sheep;
    our @ISA = qw(Animal);
    sub sound { "baaaah" }
  }
```

The Mouse package is slightly different because of the extra quietness:

```
  { package Mouse;
    our @ISA = qw(Animal);
    sub sound { "squeak" }
    sub speak {
      my $class = shift;
      $class->SUPER::speak;
      print "[but you can barely hear it!]\n";
    }
  }
```

Now, enter the interactive part of the program:

```
  my @barnyard = ( );
  {
    print "enter an animal (empty to finish): ";
    chomp(my $animal = <STDIN>);
    $animal = ucfirst lc $animal;                # canonicalize
    last unless $animal =~ /^(Cow|Horse|Sheep|Mouse)$/;
    push @barnyard, $animal;
    redo;
  }

  foreach my $beast (@barnyard) {
    $beast->speak;
  }
```

This code uses a simple check, via a pattern match, to ensure that the user doesn't enter Alpaca or another unavailable animal, because doing so will crash the program. In Chapter 9, you learned about the isa method, which lets you check more simply whether something is an available animal, even allowing for the possibility that it is an animal that was added to the program after the check was written.

Exercise 2

Here's one way to do it. First, create the base class of LivingCreature with a single speak method:

```
  use strict;
  { package LivingCreature;
    sub speak {
      my $class = shift;
      if (@_) {                    # something to say
        print "a $class goes '@_'\n";
      } else {
```

```
        print "a $class goes ", $class->sound, "\n";
      }
    }
  }
```

A person is a living creature, so define the derived class here:

```
{ package Person;
  our @ISA = qw(LivingCreature);
  sub sound { "hmmmm" }
}
```

The Animal class comes next, making appropriate sounds, but unable to talk (except to Dr. Doolittle):

```
{ package Animal;
  our @ISA = qw(LivingCreature);
  sub sound { die "all Animals should define a sound" }
  sub speak {
    my $class = shift;
    die "animals can't talk!" if @_;
    $class->SUPER::speak;
  }
}
{ package Cow;
  our @ISA = qw(Animal);
  sub sound { "moooo" }
}
{ package Horse;
  our @ISA = qw(Animal);
  sub sound { "neigh" }
}
{ package Sheep;
  our @ISA = qw(Animal);
  sub sound { "baaaah" }
}
{ package Mouse;
  our @ISA = qw(Animal);
  sub sound { "squeak" }
  sub speak {
    my $class = shift;
    $class->SUPER::speak;
    print "[but you can barely hear it!]\n";
  }
}
```

Finally, have the person speak:

```
Person->speak;                    # just hmms
Person->speak("Hello, world!");
```

Notice that the main speak routine has now moved into the LivingCreature class, which means you don't need to write it again to use it in Person. In Animal, though, you need to check that to ensure an Animal won't try to speak before calling SUPER:: speak.

Although it's not the way the assignment was written, you can get a similar result if you choose to make Person a subclass of Animal. (In that case, LivingCreature would presumably be needed as a parent class for an eventual Plant class.) Of course, since an Animal can't speak, how can a Person? The answer is that Person::speak would have to handle its parameters, if any, before or after (or instead of) calling SUPER::speak.

Which would be the better way to implement this? It all depends upon what classes you'll need in the future and how you'll use them. If you expect to add features to Animal that would be needed for Person, it makes sense for Person to inherit from Animal. If the two are nearly completely distinct, and nearly anything that a Person has in common with an Animal is common to all LivingCreatures, it's probably better to avoid the extra inheritance step. The ability to design a suitable inheritance structure is a crucial talent for any OOP programmer.

In fact, you may find that after developing the code one way, you'll want to "refactor" the code a different way. This is common with OOP. However, it's very important to have enough testing in place to ensure that you don't break things while you're moving them around.

Answer for Chapter 9

Exercise

First, start the Animal package:

```
use strict;
{ package Animal;
  use Carp qw(croak);
```

And now for the constructor:

```
## constructors
sub named {
  ref(my $class = shift) and croak "class name needed";
  my $name = shift;
  my $self = { Name => $name, Color => $class->default_color };
  bless $self, $class;
}
```

Now, for virtual methods: the methods that should be overridden in a subclass. Perl doesn't require virtual methods to be declared in the base class, but it's nice as a documentation item.

```
## backstops (should be overridden)
sub default_color { "brown" }
sub sound { croak "subclass must define a sound" }
```

Next comes the methods that work with either a class or an instance:

```
## class/instance methods
sub speak {
  my $either = shift;
  print $either->name, " goes ", $either->sound, "\n";
}
sub name {
  my $either = shift;
  ref $either
    ? $either->{Name}
    : "an unnamed $either";
}
sub color {
  my $either = shift;
  ref $either
    ? $either->{Color}
    : $either->default_color;
}
```

Finally, the methods that work only for the particular instance:

```
## instance-only methods
sub set_name {
  ref(my $self = shift) or croak "instance variable needed";
  $self->{Name} = shift;
}
sub set_color {
  ref(my $self = shift) or croak "instance variable needed";
  $self->{Color} = shift;
}
}
```

Now that you have your abstract base class, define some concrete classes that can have instances:

```
{ package Horse;
  our @ISA = qw(Animal);
  sub sound { "neigh" }
}
{ package Sheep;
  our @ISA = qw(Animal);
  sub color { "white" }     # override the default color
  sub sound { "baaaah" }    # no Silence of the Lambs
}
```

Finally, a few lines of code to test your classes:

```
my $tv_horse = Horse->named("Mr. Ed");
$tv_horse->set_name("Mister Ed");
$tv_horse->set_color("grey");
print $tv_horse->name, " is ", $tv_horse->color, "\n";
print Sheep->name, " colored ", Sheep->color, " goes ", Sheep->sound, "\n";
```

Answer for Chapter 10

Exercise

First, start the class:

```
{ package RaceHorse;
  our @ISA = qw(Horse);
```

Next, use a simple dbmopen to associate %STANDINGS with permanent storage:

```
dbmopen (our %STANDINGS, "standings", 0666)
  or die "Cannot access standings dbm: $!";
```

When a new RaceHorse is named, either pull the existing standings from the database or invent zeroes for everything:

```
sub named { # class method
  my $self = shift->SUPER::named(@_);
  my $name = $self->name;
  my @standings = split ' ', $STANDINGS{$name} || "0 0 0 0";
  @$self{qw(wins places shows losses)} = @standings;
  $self;
}
```

When the RaceHorse is destroyed, the standings are updated:

```
sub DESTROY { # instance method, automatically invoked
  my $self = shift;
  $STANDINGS{$self->name} = "@$self{qw(wins places shows losses)}";
  $self->SUPER::DESTROY;
}
```

Finally, the instance methods are defined:

```
## instance methods:
sub won { shift->{wins}++; }
sub placed { shift->{places}++; }
sub showed { shift->{shows}++; }
sub lost { shift->{losses}++; }
sub standings {
  my $self = shift;
  join ", ", map "$self->{$_} $_", qw(wins places shows losses);
}
}
```

Answer for Chapter 11

Exercise

```
use IO::File;
my %output_handles;
while (<>) {
```

```
  unless (/^(\S+):/) {
    warn "ignoring the line with missing name: $_";
    next;
  }
  my $name = lc $1;
  my $handle = $output_handles{$name} ||=
    IO::File->open(">$name.info") || die "Cannot create $name.info: $!";
  print $handle $_;
}
```

At the beginning of the while loop, use a pattern to extract the person's name from the data line, issuing a warning if that's not found.

Once you have the name, force it to lowercase so that an entry for "Maryann" will get filed in the same place as one for "MaryAnn." This is also handy for naming the files, as the next statement shows.

The first time through the loop, the filehandle must be created. Let's see how to do that. The || operator has a higher precedence than the assignment, so it is evaluated first; the program will die if the file can't be created. The ||= operator assigns the filehandle to the hash, and the = operator passes it to $handle as well.

The next time you have the same name in $name, the ||= operator kicks in. Remember that $gilligan ||= $anything is effectively like $gilligan = $gilligan || $anything. If the variable on the left is a false value (such as undef), it's replaced by the value on the right, but if it's true (such as a filehandle), the value on the right won't even be evaluated. Thus, since the hash already has a value for that person's name, the hash's value is used and assigned directly to $handle without having to (re-)create the file.

It wasn't necessary to code the castaways' names into this program, because they will be read in as data. This is good because any additional castaway won't require having to rewrite the program. If someone's name is accidentally misspelled, however, it puts some of their data into a new file under the wrong name.

Answer for Chapter 12

Exercise

The module Oogaboogoo/date.pm looks like this:

```
package Oogaboogoo::date;
use strict;
use Exporter;
our @ISA = qw(Exporter);
our @EXPORT = qw(day mon);

my @day = qw(ark dip wap sen pop sep kir);
my @mon = qw(diz pod bod rod sip wax lin sen kun fiz nap dep);

sub day {
```

```perl
    my $num = shift @_;
    die "$num is not a valid day number"
      unless $num >= 0 and $num <= 6;
    $day[$num];
}

sub mon {
  my $num = shift @_;
  die "$num is not a valid month number"
    unless $num >= 0 and $num <= 11;
  $mon[$num];
}

1;
```

The main program now looks like this:

```perl
use strict;
use Oogaboogoo::date qw(day mon);

my($sec, $min, $hour, $mday, $mon, $year, $wday) = localtime;
my $day_name = day($wday);
my $mon_name = mon($mon);
$year += 1900;
print "Today is $day_name, $mon_name $mday, $year.\n";
```

Answers for Chapters 13–15

These complete projects are far too complex to represent completely here. We hope readers of this book will share their solutions with each other on the Internet. Try a search on the Web for the phrase "Perl Alpaca book LPORM answers." You can also use that phrase on the web page where you offer your solutions for downloading. To help anyone who finds your page, include links from your page to any other solutions that look interesting to you.

We search the Web from time to time, and so we may visit your site and look at your results. If we especially like your solution to the halting problem, we'll be sure to let you know.

Index

Symbols

& (ampersand), 62, 138
@_ array
    accessing instance data, 101
    changes reflected, 19
    creating, 18
    dereferencing and, 21
    nested data structures, 23
    passing uninterrupted, 97
    references and scoping, 31
    removing items from, 4
\ (backslash), 19, 26, 62
: (colon), 10
, (comma), 39
{} (curly braces)
    anonymous hash constructors, 38
    arrays and, 20
    coderefs and, 63
    dereferencing, 25
    dropping, 21, 22
    hashes and, 26
    indirect object syntax and, 118
:: (double colon), 13, 140
= operator, 195
?: operator, 103
|| operator, 195
||= operator, 195
() (parentheses), 37, 62, 75
+ (plus sign), 40, 114
# (pound sign), 44, 168
; (semicolon), 40, 69
<=> (spaceship operator), 78
[] (square brackets), 36, 37

_ (underscore), 13
$@ variable, 6, 8

A

absent import lists, 138
abstract methods, 131
accessors
    AUTOLOAD method and, 129, 130
    Class::MethodMaker module, 130–132
anonymous arrays
    complex data and, 59
    creating directly, 35–38
    defined, 32
    hash references and, 38
    square brackets and, 36
anonymous hash
    creating, 38–40
    filesystem capture example, 84
anonymous subroutines, 65, 67
API (Application Programming
    Interface), 105
archiving, 148
arguments (see parameters)
array reference
    anonymous array constructors and,
        36, 37
    arrows and, 25, 26
    blessing, 114
    curly braces and, 21, 22
    dereferencing, 20, 21, 23, 32
    efficient sorting example, 80
    empty arrays and, 41
    features, 19, 20

We'd like to hear your suggestions for improving our indexes. Send email to *index@oreilly.com*.

array reference (*continued*)
  hashes into, 59
  IO::File objects and, 134
  modifying, 22, 23
  nested data structures, 23–24
  Schwartzian Transform, 81
ARRAY(0x1a2b3c), 19
arrays
  curly braces, 20
  dereferencing and, 23, 32
  modifying, 22, 23
  nested data structures and, 23
  ordered lists and, 17
  package names and, 13
  referencing, 19, 20, 21
  scalars and, 17
  scoping considerations, 36
  (see also anonymous arrays)
arrows
  drop arrow rule, 25
  hash references and, 26, 27
  method invocation arrow, 90, 91, 97, 118
AUTOLOAD method
  accessors and, 129, 130
  functionality, 128, 129
  inheritance and, 93
$AUTOLOAD variable, 128
AutoLoader core module, 129
autovivification
  hash references and, 42–44
  process defined, 40–42

B

backstop method, 106, 126
basename subroutine (File::Basename), 137
BEGIN block
  importing subroutines, 141
  purpose, 74
  setting constants, 143
  setting paths, 142
  use list and, 140
  use operation and, 172
behavior
  classes and, 90
  instances and, 100
  passing as parameter, 68
  subroutine references and, 61
  testing with isa and can methods, 127, 128
blessed references
  indirect object syntax and, 118
  instances as, 100, 101, 105

isa method and, 127
nested object destruction, 114
ref operator and, 103
returning, 102
block form
  grep operator, 53
  map operator, 55

C

callbacks
  accessing variables, 69, 71
  find( ) function and, 68, 69
  invoking subroutines multiple times, 72
  subroutine references and, 67, 68
can method (UNIVERSAL), 127, 128
can_ok function (Test::More), 170
catfile method (File::Spec), 139
CGI module, 147
Changes file, 151
class methods
  building instances, 102
  File::Spec module and, 139
  instance methods and, 101
  OO modules and, 140
  restricting to, 110
class variables, 121–122
classes
  accessors and, 131
  defined, 90
  instances and, 100
  methods working with, 103
  UNIVERSAL class and, 126
  virtual methods and, 192
Class::MethodMaker module, 130–132
closure variables, 73–75
closures
  functionality, 68–70
  lexical variables and, 73
  persistence and, 74
  scope and, 73
cmp operator, 78
cmp_ok routine (Test::More), 170
code
  decoupling, 21
  reusability of, 95, 137
  testing coverage, 165
  ways to share, 4–11
  (see also OOP)
code references
  AUTOLOAD method and, 129
  overview, 61–75
collisions, namespace, 11–12, 139

comments, 44, 168
compile phase
  AUTOLOAD and, 128
  BEGIN keyword and, 75
  declarations during, 74
  use base and, 94
complex data structures (see data structures)
composition, inheritance versus, 120
Comprehensive Perl Archive Network (see
    CPAN)
conditional tests, 172
constants, setting, 143
constructors
  anonymous array, 36, 37, 59
  anonymous hash, 38, 39, 40
  creating instances, 102
  inheriting, 102, 103
  url subroutine, 146
copyright notices, 151
core modules, 13, 102, 129
CPAN (Comprehensive Perl Archive
    Network)
  contributing to, 175–179
  version numbers and, 153
current directory
  find( ) function and, 68, 69
  @INC array and, 9
  search path and, 9, 68
  testing and, 174

D

data
  accessing for instances, 101
  selecting, 58, 59
  storing, 51–53, 74, 194
  viewing with Data::Dumper, 50, 51
  viewing with debugger, 45–49
data structures
  looping and, 34, 35
  manipulating, 45–59
  nested, 23, 24, 32–34
  recursively defined, 82–85
  references to anonymous, 30
  references to subroutines, 61
Data::Dumper module, 50, 51, 85
daylight savings time (DST), 76
dbmopen function, 194
debugging
  Changes file and, 151
  enabling warnings during, 183

viewing complex data, 45–49
  x command, 46, 50
delegation, 120
dereferencing
  array references, 20, 21, 23, 32
  coderefs, 62, 63
  hash references, 26
  lexical variables and, 69
DESTROY method
  inheritance and, 117
  nested objects, 114
  purpose, 112, 113
destructors
  class variables and, 122
  IO::File objects and, 134
  nested objects example, 114–117
direct object syntax, 118, 119
directories
  represented as hashes, 82
  separating with colon, 10
  t files and, 166
dirname subroutine (File::Basename), 137
distributions
  alternate installation locations, 159
  announcing CPAN modules, 178
  copyrights and licensing, 151
  embedded documentation, 154–157
  Exporter module, 152
  h2xs tool, 149
  make dist and, 162
  Makefile.PL, 158–159
  modules within, 152–154
  POD format, 155–157
  preparing, 176, 177
  qw( ) lists, 152
  template files, 149–151
  testing, 160–161, 164
  Test::More module, 168–172
  Test::Simple module, 167, 168
  uploading to CPAN, 177, 178
  version numbers, 153, 177
do operator, 6–8
documentation
  distribution considerations, 148
  embedded for distribution, 154–157
  testing and, 165
drop arrow rule, 25
Dumper subroutine, 50

E

empty import lists, 138
encapsulation, object, 108
END blocks, 113
_ _END_ _ marker, 154
eval function, 5, 6
@EXPORT variable, 144, 145, 153
Exporter module
    distributions, 152
    importing with, 143, 146
    package variables, 144
export_fail method (Exporter), 146
exporting
    OO modules and, 140, 145–147, 153
    symbols, 152
@EXPORT_OK variable, 144, 145, 153
export_to_level method (Exporter), 146
expression form
    grep operator, 53
    map operator, 55
extending
    class variables, 121
    subroutines, 119
    superclass methods, 117
ExtUtils::MakeMaker module, 158

F

File::Basename module, 137, 143
File::Find module
    features, 67, 68–70
    returning coderefs, 75
filehandles
    instance variables, 116
    ok function (Test::More) and, 173
    package names and, 13
    || operator and, 195
    references to, 133–135
    storing in a hash, 195
    temporary files, 112
fileparse subroutine (File::Basename),
        137, 143
files
    distribution templates, 149–151
    File::Spec module, 138
    find subroutine, 68–70
    finding timestamps, 75
    parsing specifications, 137
File::Spec module, 138
filesystems
    capturing information about, 82–85
    walking through hierarchy, 67, 68

find subroutine (File::Find), 67, 68–70
friend classes, 120, 132

G

garbage collection, 35
getters
    AUTOLOAD method and, 129, 130
    creating easily, 130–132
    doubling as setters, 109, 110
    encapsulation and, 108
    optimizing, 109
glob operator, 86, 130, 134
global variables
    data destruction and, 113
    package variables as, 15
    scope and, 73
grep operator
    filehandles and, 135
    functionality, 53–55
    indices and, 78
    indirection and, 57
    scalar context and, 17, 53
    selecting complex data, 59
    (see also Schwartzian Transform)

H

h2xs tool
    distributions and, 149
    Makefile.PL and, 158
    multiple test scripts and, 173
hash reference
    anonymous hash constructors, 38
    autovivification and, 42–44
    Data::Dumper example, 50
    debugging example, 46, 48, 49
    dereferencing, 26
    features, 26–28
    filesystem capture example, 84
    object destruction, 112
    as parameters, 28
    as return values, 83
HASH(0x1a2b3c), 28
hashes
    directories as, 82
    instances and, 105
    map operator and, 55
    package names and, 13
    references and, 19, 59
    scalars and, 17
    storing filehandles, 195
    (see also anonymous hash)
hexadecimal memory address, 19, 28

I

importing
    custom routines, 147
    Exporter module and, 143
    File::Basename module and, 138
    -nosticky option, 147
    subroutines, 141, 145
    use operation and, 140
@INC array
    require operator and, 9–11
    use operation and, 141
indices, sorting with, 78, 79
indirect object notation, 118–119
indirection
    applying, 56–58
    sorting indices, 79
inheritance
    code reusability through, 95
    composition versus, 120
    constructors and, 102, 103
    DESTROY method and, 117
    isa method testing, 127
    @ISA variable and, 93
    method invocation and, 92, 93
    multiple inheritance, 132
installation (of modules)
    alternate library locations, 162
    alternate locations, 159
    distribution considerations, 148
instance methods
    APIs and, 105
    class methods and, 101
    invoking, 100, 101
    Math::BigInt module, 139
    OO modules and, 140
    parameters and, 105
    restricting to, 110
instance variables
    defined, 100
    filehandles as, 116
    hash keys, 105
    object destruction and, 112
    in subclasses, 119, 121
instances
    accessors and, 131
    blessed references and, 100, 101
    building, 102
    defined, 99, 100
    hashes and, 105
    isa method testing, 127
    methods working with, 103

interfaces
    distribution considerations, 148
    File::Basename module, 137
    File::Spec module, 138
    maintenance considerations, 132
    version numbers and, 153
IO::File class, 133, 134
is function (Test::More), 169, 174
@ISA variable
    features, 93, 94
    inheritance hierarchies and, 126
    multiple inheritance, 132
isa method (UNIVERSAL), 127, 128
isa_ok function (Test::More), 170
isnt function (Test::More), 169
iteration versus recursion, 82

K

key/value pairs, 40

L

lexical variables
    closures and, 69, 73
    data destruction and, 113
    defined, 6
    @ISA and, 93
    packages and, 15
    reference longevity, 31
    subroutine references, 69, 70, 73
libraries
    alternate installation locations, 159, 162
    loading only once, 8
    search path for, 9
licensing, 151
like function (Test::More), 170
lists
    absent import lists, 138
    qw( ) list, 138, 152
    sorted list, 184
looping (code structure), 49, 75
looping (data structure), 34, 35

M

maintenance considerations, 132
make dist, 162
make install, 161
make test, 160–161, 164, 168
Makefile.PL
    controlling distribution, 158–159
    PREFIX=option, 159, 162
    test harness, 160, 166, 167, 169
    testing and, 177

MANIFEST file, 149, 150, 177
map operator
    functionality, 53–56
    indirection and, 58
    scalar context, 55
    selecting complex data, 59
    (see also Schwartzian Transform)
Math::BigInt module, 139
member variables, 100, 105
memory addresses, 19, 28
memory management, 34–35, 124
meta-variables, 121
methods
    abstract methods, 131
    getters doubling as setters, 109
    inheritance and, 92, 93
    instances and, 100, 101
    invocation arrow, 90, 91, 97, 118
    overriding, 94–96
    parameters and, 91, 92, 104, 105
    restricting, 110
    superclasses, 117
    UNIVERSAL class and, 126
    working with classes, 103
    (see also class methods; instance methods)
modules
    announcing, 178
    core modules, 13, 102, 129
    distributions and, 149, 152–154
    overview, 137–147
    (see also packages)
my variables, 6, 14

N

namespaces
    packages as separators, 12–14
    problems with collisions, 11–12, 139
nested entities
    data structures, 23, 24, 32–34
    element references, 25
    object destruction, 114–117
new method
    creating objects, 102
    indirect object notation, 118
    Math::BigInt module, 139
numbers
    sorting, 77, 78
    testing equality, 169

O

object-oriented programming (see OOP)
objects
    bless operator and, 100
    as blessed references, 105
    creating, 102
    destruction of, 112–124
    encapsulation of, 108
    filehandles and, 133
    instances and, 100
    structure considerations, 106
    testing with isa and can methods, 127,
        128
ok function (Test::Simple), 167, 173
OO (object-oriented) modules
    exporting, 153
    exporting and, 145–147
    non-OO versus, 140
    Test::More module, 170
OOP (object-oriented programming)
    File::Spec module, 138
    inheritance structures and, 192
    overview, 88–98
    versus non-OOP, 140
ordered lists, 17
our variables, 94
overriding
    methods, 94–96
    superclass methods, 117
    UNIVERSAL class methods, 126

P

packages
    global variables, 15, 73
    @ISA variable and, 93
    lexicals and, 15
    main program in, 14
    as namespace separators, 12–14
    naming considerations, 13, 90
    scope of directives, 14, 15
    (see also modules)
parameters
    @_, 97
    adding to methods, 104, 105
    callbacks and, 71
    hash references as, 28
    instance methods and, 100
    instances as, 101
    method invocation and, 91, 92
    passing to superclasses, 120
    returning updated values, 107

shifting, 93, 97
(see also return values)
parent-child relationships, 124
parsing
file specifications, 137
shifting style, 4, 18
passing by reference (see references)
PATH environment variable, 9
paths, searching for installed
modules/libraries, 141, 143
PAUSE (Perl Authors Upload Server)
ID, 176, 177
perl command
-d option, 46
-I option, 11, 162
-M option, 162
PREFIX= option (Makefile.PL), 159, 162
-V command line option, 9
-V:make, 158
-w option, 119, 183
PERL5LIB environment variable, 10
perl-packrats mailing list, 175
.pl (Perl Library) extension, 7
.plx (Perl Executable) extension, 7
.pm (Perl Module) extension, 140
POD format, 155–157
prefixes, explicit, 12
PREREQ_PM setting (Makefiles), 159
programs
behaviors of, 61
compile phase, 74
object destruction and, 113
run phase, 74
sharing code, 4–11
whitespace, 20, 40
(see also OOP)
properties, instances and, 100
push function, 10

Q

qw( ) list, 138, 152

R

README file, 150, 151, 177
recursively defined data, 82–85
ref operator, 103, 110
reference counting
closures and, 70
defined, 30
garbage collection and, 35
memory management and, 34–35

nested data structures and, 32–34
subroutine reference example, 73
weak references and, 123
references
bless operator, 100
destruction and, 123
to filehandles, 133–135
hierarchical data and, 82
instances and, 100, 103, 105
named subroutines, 61–75
object destruction and, 112
overview, 17–28
return values, 102
as scalars, 183
scoping and, 30–44
weak references, 122–124
(see also array reference; blessed
references; dereferencing; hash
reference)
require operator
functionality, 8, 9
@INC and, 9–11
syntax errors and, 8
use operation and, 140
require_version method (Exporter), 146
return values
bless operator and, 102
coderefs as, 75
hash references, 83
required files, 141
subroutine references, 70
undef example, 83
updated parameters, 107
(see also parameters)
run phase
BEGIN keyword and, 75
storage allocation, 74

S

s command (debugger), 46
scalars
anonymous, 70
curly braces and, 63
filehandles and, 134
hash references and, 39
indirect object syntax, 118
isa method and, 127
package names and, 13
references and, 19, 183
single values and, 17

Schwartzian Transform
    dictionary order, 86
    performance, 188
    sorting and, 81
scope
    do operator and, 6
    global variables and, 73
    references and, 30–44
scripts
    alternate installation locations, 159
    complex tests, 173
search path, 9, 68
SelfLoader core module, 129
setters
    AUTOLOAD method and, 129, 130
    creating, 106–108, 130–132
    encapsulation and, 108
    getters doubling as, 109, 110
    optimizing, 109
    restricting methods, 110
shifting
    @_ array, 18
    argument parsing, 4, 18
    arguments, 93, 97
    closure variables, 73
    example eliminating, 21
smoke tests, 178
sorting
    dictionary order, 86
    efficient, 79–81
    glob operator, 86
    with indices, 78, 79
    review of, 77, 78
    Schwartzian Transform, 81
    sort blocks, 77
    sorted list, 184
spaceship operator, 78
sqrt function, 165
static local variables, 73–75
STDERR filehandle, 173
STDOUT filehandle, 173
Storable module, 51–53
storing data, 51–53, 74, 194
strings (see text strings)
subclasses
    abstract methods and, 131
    instance variables in, 119, 121
subroutine references, 61–75
subroutines
    custom import routines, 147
    extending, 119
    importing, 141, 145

isa called as, 128
modules and, 137
out of scope variables and, 73
package names and, 13
referencing, 61–65
syntax errors and, 6
(see also closures)
SUPER pseudo-class, 97
superclasses, 97, 117, 120
symbols, 143, 152
syntax errors, 6, 8
system performance, 132

T
t directory, 166
"take a reference to" operator, 19, 26, 62
template files, 149–151
temporary files
    data destruction and, 112, 116, 117
    STDOUT and, 174
testing
    code coverage, 165
    conditional tests, 172
    distributions and, 148, 160–161
    inequality, 169
    isa and can methods, 127, 128
    Makefile.PL and, 177
    multiple test scripts, 173
    numeric equality, 169
    pound-sign comments and, 168
    smoke tests, 178
    sqrt function, 165
    test harness, 160, 166, 167, 169
    use operation, 171
    writing to STDOUT and STDERR, 173
testing expression (of map or grep), 53, 55
Test::More module, 168–172, 173
Test::Simple module, 167, 168
TEST_VERBOSE option (make test), 168
text strings
    cmp operator, 78
    like function, 170
    ref operator and, 103
    sorting, 77
timestamps, 75
TODO blocks, 172
$TODO variable, 172

U

undef (value)
  autovivification and, 42
  filesystem capture example, 83
  ref operator and, 103
  variables with value of, 74
  weak references and, 124
unimport method (Exporter), 146
UNIVERSAL class
  inheritance and, 93
  purpose of, 126
  utility methods, 127, 128
unshift function, 10, 142
URIs (universal resource identifiers), 146
URI::URL module, 146
url subroutine (URI::URL), 146
use base, 94
use CGI, 147
use lib, 142, 162
use operation, 140–141, 153, 171, 172
use strict, 90, 93

V

variables
  bless operator, 100
  callbacks and, 69, 71
  class variables, 121–122
  closure variables, 73–75
  filehandles and, 133
  global variables, 15, 73, 113
  member variables, 100, 105
  memory addresses of, 19
  meta-variables, 121
  modules and, 137
  my variables, 6, 14
  our variables, 94
  out of scope, 69, 70, 72, 73
  package names, 90
  reference removal and, 31, 32
  as repository of values, 61
  static local, 73–75
  (see also instance variables; lexical
    variables; scalars)
version numbers, 153, 177
$VERSION variable, 162
viewing data
  Data::Dumper, 50, 51
  with debugger, 45–49
void context, 107, 108

W

wantarray function, 107
warnings, enabling, 8, 183
weak references, 122–124
WeakRef module, 123
When, 123
whitespace, 20, 40
working directory (see current directory)
WriteMakefile subroutine
    (ExtUtils::MakeMaker), 158
writing distributions, 148–163

X

x command (debugger), 46, 50

About the Authors

Randal L. Schwartz is a two-decade veteran of the software industry. He is skilled in software design, system administration, security, technical writing, and training. Randal has coauthored the "must-have" standards: *Programming Perl*, *Learning Perl*, *Learning Perl for Win32 Systems*, and *Effective Perl Programming*, and is a regular columnist for *WebTechniques*, *PerformanceComputing*, *SysAdmin*, and *Linux* magazines. He is also a frequent contributor to the Perl newsgroups and has moderated *comp.lang.perl.announce* since its inception. His offbeat humor and technical mastery have reached legendary proportions worldwide (but he probably started some of those legends himself). Randal's desire to give back to the Perl community inspired him to help create and provide initial funding for The Perl Institute. He is also a founding board member of the Perl Mongers (*perl.org*), the worldwide Perl grassroots advocacy organization. Since 1985, Randal has owned and operated Stonehenge Consulting Services, Inc. Randal can be reached for comment at *merlyn@stonehenge.com* or (503) 777-0095, and welcomes questions on Perl and other related topics.

Tom Phoenix has been working in the field of education since 1982. After more than 13 years of dissections, explosions, work with interesting animals, and high-voltage sparks during his work at a science museum, he started teaching Perl classes for Stonehenge Consulting Services, where he's worked since 1996. Since then, he has traveled to many interesting locations, so you might see him soon at a Perl Mongers' meeting. When he has time, he answers questions on Usenet's *comp.lang.perl.misc* and *comp.lang.perl.moderated* newsgroups, and contributes to the development and usefulness of Perl. Besides his work with Perl, Perl hackers, and related topics, Tom spends his time on amateur cryptography and speaking Esperanto. His home is in Portland, Oregon.

Colophon

Our look is the result of reader comments, our own experimentation, and feedback from distribution channels. Distinctive covers complement our distinctive approach to technical topics, breathing personality and life into potentially dry subjects.

The animal on the cover of *Learning Perl Objects, References, and Modules* is an alpaca (*Lama pacos*). The alpaca is a member of the South American camelid family, which is closely related to the more familiar Asian and African camels. South American camelids also include the llama, the vicuna, and the guanaco. The alpaca is smaller (36 inches at the withers) than a llama, but larger than its other relations. Ninety-nine percent of the world's approximately three million alpacas are found in Peru, Bolivia, and Chile.

The evolution of the wild vicuna into the domestic alpaca began between six and seven thousand years ago. The specialized breeding of alpacas for fiber production wasn't developed until around 500 B.C. The Incas developed the alpaca into the two distinct fleece types, the Huacaya (pronounced wa-kai-ya) and the less common Suri. The main difference between the two types of alpacas is the fiber they produce. The Huacaya fleece has crimp or wave; the Suri fleece is silky and lustrous and has no crimp. Alpacas are prized for their fleece, which is as soft as cashmere and warmer, lighter, and stronger than wool. Alpaca fleece comes in more colors than that of any other fiber-producing animal (approximately 22 basic colors with many variations and blends).

The lifespan of the alpaca is about 20 years. Gestation is 11.5 months, producing one offspring, or cria, every 14 to 15 months. The alpaca is a modified ruminant, not only eating less grass than most other animals but converting it to energy very efficiently. Unlike true ruminants, they have three compartments in their stomach, not four, and can thus survive in areas unsuitable to other domesticated animals. Alpacas are gentle and don't bite or butt. Even if they did, without incisors, horns, hoofs, or claws, they would do little damage.

Mary Anne Weeks Mayo was the production editor and proofreader, and Ann Schirmer was the copyeditor for *Learning Perl Objects, References, and Modules*. Matt Hutchinson and Claire Cloutier provided quality control. Jamie Peppard provided production assistance. Lucie Haskins wrote the index.

Ellie Volckhausen designed the cover of this book, based on a series design by Edie Freedman. The cover image is a 19th-century engraving from *Animate Creations*, Volume II. Emma Colby produced the cover layout with QuarkXPress 4.1 using Adobe's ITC Garamond font.

David Futato designed the interior layout. This book was converted by Andrew Savikas to FrameMaker 5.5.6 with a format conversion tool created by Erik Ray, Jason McIntosh, Neil Walls, and Mike Sierra that uses Perl and XML technologies. The text font is Linotype Birka; the heading font is Adobe Myriad Condensed; and the code font is LucasFont's TheSans Mono Condensed. The illustrations that appear in the book were produced by Robert Romano and Jessamyn Read using Macromedia FreeHand 9 and Adobe Photoshop 6. This colophon was compiled by Mary Anne Weeks Mayo.